Assessing Visually Handicapped People

An Introduction to Test Procedures

Michael J. Tobin

David Fulton Publishers

London

David Fulton Publishers Ltd
2 Barbon Close, London WC1N 3JX

First published in Great Britain by
David Fulton Publishers 1994

Reprinted 1997

Note: The right of the contributors to be identified as the authors of this work has been asserted by him in accordance with the Copyright, Designs and Patents Act 1988.

Copyright © Michael J Tobin

British Library Cataloguing in Publication Data

A catalogue record for this book is available from the British Library

ISBN 1-85346-295-0

Designed by Almac Ltd., London
Typeset by Action Typesetting Limited, Gloucester
Printed in Great Britain by Antony Rowe Ltd., Chippenham, Wiltshire

Contents

Tables

Figures

Preface

This book describes and evaluates assessment procedures for those professional workers whose concerns are at the 'handicap' end of a continuum that is characterized by the terms impairment, disability and handicap. The World Health Organization (WHO) has sought to bring some order into the terminology of disablement (*vide*, for example, Wood (1980)), with 'disablement' itself being recommended as the general term to cover all aspects of the phenomenon. In the WHO model, impairment refers to some loss or abnormality of an organ or of some part of the physiology or anatomy of the organism. Disability is then one of the possible consequences of an impairment and is conceived of as lack of ability to function within the range considered normal for most human beings. Handicap is in its turn a possible consequence of a disability.

Impairment may be seen as a concept and a label that operates at the level of the organ; disability at the level of the person; and handicap at the level of the person-in-society. For example, colour blindness is an impairment in the eye's cone receptors. This impairment results in the individual being unable to distinguish certain colours, but uncomplicated colour blindness is regarded as a disability of little clinical and practical significance. For an Eskimo hunter with perfect visual acuity, colour blindness may not have any significant handicapping consequences. If he wished to change his lifestyle and become an airline pilot, then his colour blindness would constitute an insuperable handicap.

In this book, the concern is not with the visual impairment, which is properly the concern of ophthalmologists and other medically qualified specialists; it is, rather, with means of assessing the educational, vocational and social handicaps that may follow from, or be associated with, visual impairments and disabilities. It is aimed to be of use to the teachers and advisers who work with blind and partially sighted pupils; to the educational and clinical psychologists who assess, and who devise teaching, therapeutic and counselling programmes for visually disabled children and adults; and to the specialist rehabilitation officers and social workers who have day-to-day responsibility for their well-being.

Many of the assessment procedures that are to be examined are commercially published, standardized tests. One of the criticisms of the use of such instruments, whether in relation to handicapped or non-handicapped people, has been that they have led to the assignment of a permanent quotient or a label to the person being assessed, and that this in turn has served to limit the expectations of what can be achieved or attempted. The pernicious effects of this once-only testing cannot, however, be attributed to some inherent defects in standardized tests as such. They are due rather to a mis-reading of the purposes of the tests, and to a mis-use of the results and their possible developmental implications. A single 'snapshot' assessment can show where a child is at that precise moment in relation to what is expected or normally found among children of the same age; it can also suggest that his level of functioning may be more akin to that of a younger or older child. What it cannot do with any certainty is to indicate that he will always be at a specific level of delay or advancement in relation to his age-mates.

For the visually handicapped child, these 'one-off' assessments can be even more problematical. The inter-relatedness of most human skills, especially in the earliest years, can result in an overall level of retardation, due entirely to one or two specific areas of deficit. For example, congenitally blind infants are often, but by no means always, slow to crawl, some of them omitting this stage of locomotor development altogether. Their failure to do this, or to do it within the age-range considered normal for the fully sighted, may well be associated with apparent lack of interest in feeling and handling small objects and the surfaces and textures of furniture, in reaching for sound-making toys, and in searching for things dropped from their grasp. Crawling itself is probably triggered by the sight of familiar objects beyond arm's reach, given of course the necessary physiological maturation. In the absence of visual incentives to crawl, the baby may remain seated and is thus effectively debarred from chance encounters with objects in his immediate environment. The opportunities for manipulation and palpation of new shapes are thus severely reduced in number, as are the opportunities for learning about cause and effect relationships. The rewarding and reinforcing consequences of these actions and insights are therefore also absent. The effect is often a widespread, but temporary, deficit as measured by the test.

A similar phenomenon is sometimes observed in the development of expressive language. For the sighted child, the ability to monitor the mother's line of gaze, and thus 'know' what is in her mind, is an important pre-cursor of the emergence of language. This direct, visually mediated, sharing of experience is not available to blind infants and their families. Nor is the ability to imitate the mother's lip, teeth and tongue movements, movements that are typically somewhat exaggerated by the mother to encourage the sighted child to copy the correct positions of the mouth for the sounds of the native language. Again, a massive, overall deficit in language development may be registered by a test administered once only.

At an older age, the tests used for assessing reading progress have been standardized for fully sighted or, occasionally, visually handicapped populations. Although it is never explicitly stated, there is also the assumption that all readers have been through the normal process of reading tuition and practice. However, some of the children with a visual disability for whom an assessment is required have not been through that 'normal' process. Their blindness may have had a late onset, after some progress has already been made with print reading; the change-over to a tactile reading medium may indeed be progressing satisfactorily but there is a real danger that reading speed and reading accuracy will be lagging far behind reading comprehension, resulting in reading ages and quotients substantially below those of pupils of similar age and similar ability. These deficits will probably be of temporary duration, and it is essential that the results of a single-occasion assessment of reading be interpreted with considerable caution.

With adventitiously blinded adults, such widely used tests as the Purdue Pegboard Test of Manual Dexterity can also produce results on a given administration that may grossly underestimate the subject's abilities, with the performance on a specific day being widely divergent from the 'true' level of performance. The long drawn out process of adaptation to, and acceptance of, blindness can have very deleterious, short-term effects on cognitive, perceptual and psycho-motor skills; a 'one-off' assessment, even with well-standardized instruments, must be viewed with considerable caution in relation to such newly blinded adults.

These particular defects are not inherent in standardized tests as such; they are associated, rather, with carelessness in administration and interpretation. As such, they are capable of being avoided. At the very least, they point up the importance of sustained monitoring of performance and the need for frequent reviewing of development. The child or adult suffering from a severe impairment is entitled to systematic evaluation of the educational, social and vocational handicaps that may follow from the disablement, and an essential component of such a system must be frequency and regularity in the up-dating of the records.

Ideally, the monitoring should be directed towards those critical or key areas of functioning which are known to be very susceptible to disruption by severe visual impairment, and retardation in development of which has been shown to have effects on other functions. The developmentally delayed blind infant should, therefore, perhaps be observed and tested in locomotor skills areas. The adventitiously blinded schoolchild should have his reading accuracy and reading speed monitored and then further observed to determine whether, for example, hand and finger movements are in need of improvement or whether overt explanation of complex braille contractions might be helpful. A partially sighted pupil's reading may appear to be perfectly satisfactory on a test that focuses only upon word recognition and accuracy; a test that includes rate of reading may show up problems of considerable significance in terms of the pupil's ability to maintain interest and motivation in his learning.

In so far as standardized tests are not meant for regular and frequent re-administration, and in so far as the results of a single administration to a visually handicapped individual may mis-represent his skills or competence – for one or more of the reasons already outlined – their use must be viewed with some scepticism. Conversely, those very same reasons demonstrate the need for regular and frequent monitoring of functioning to pin-point key behaviours, improvement in which can result in massive and rapid advance over a wide range of skills.

Another problem with standardized tests is that there are very few that have been designed for, and standardized on, the population of people whom we label as visually handicapped. Until recently, there were no normative data for evaluating a newly blinded adult's manual dexterity in relation to other blind people, a deficiency now made good by a study (Tobin and Greenhalgh, 1987) which allows multiple comparisons to be made – with the fully sighted, with blind men or women, and with registered blind people of differing degrees of residual vision. There are, too, whole blocks of the conventional junior and secondary school curricula for which there are no commercially produced testing procedures at all; geography and the sciences are totally unrepresented, despite the fact that they constitute especially difficult teaching/learning problems for the most severely visually impaired children.

It may be argued that too much can be made of this lack. The blind child is, after all, first and foremost a child, following the same biologically determined developmental course as sighted children and having the same general educational and social goals as his fully sighted peers. Nevertheless, there is sufficient evidence from developmental scales (such as the Reynell-Zinkin Scales), from reading tests (for example, the braille version of the Neale Analysis of Reading Ability), and from speed of visual information processing scales (such as the SIP in the British Ability Scales) to make it abundantly clear that there are important areas of functioning that are seriously affected by blindness and partial sight. There is evidence also from studies like the one carried out by Gomulicki (1961) to suggest that in early childhood there are areas of non-visual perception in which the blind child may sometimes lag behind his sighted age-peers.

The very least that should be done in the light of this evidence is to be alert to the need to interpret with care the results of the tests that have not been standardized on a population of visually handicapped children. Where there are tests that have been standardized for use with these children, there is much to be said for administering the 'sighted' versions also (where that is possible), since this can generate better levels of understanding on the part of parents and non-specialist teachers. Such a procedure can bring out quite dramatically the educationally significant implications of the visual defect or, in WHO terms, any handicapping effects.

CHAPTER 1

Definitions, Numbers and Classificatory Factors

Definitions and numbers

In the United Kingdom, a person is eligible to be registered as blind if he is 'so blind as to be unable to perform any work for which eyesight is essential' (National Assistance Act, 1948). If a person's best corrected visual acuity is such that he can see only at three metres or less what can be seen at 60 metres by someone with normal vision, then the ophthalmologist can recommend entry on to the blindness registers maintained by local social services departments. Better acuities may also lead to an individual's eligibility for registration if they are associated with restrictions in the size of the visual field. Partial sightedness is generally taken as a visual acuity of 6/18 or worse, after the best correction by lenses.

In the developed countries of the world, there is variation in the numerical indices used for classifying people as visually impaired, but they are not very different from those used in the UK. In the United States, for example, central vision of 20/200 (in feet) or less after the best correction is the criterion of legal blindness, but again a restriction in the size of the visual field can lead to classification as blind even if the central acuity is better than 20/200 (*vide* Koestler, 1976). In its 'Guidelines for programmes for the prevention of blindness', the World Health Organization (1979) uses a model in which there are in effect five categories of visual loss, ranging upwards from no light perception to measured binocular acuities between 6/60 and 6/18, this highest category corresponding to the British definition of partial sight. These approaches to the questions of definition and classification make it clear that most 'blind' people have some residual vision. They are not a homogeneous group, either in terms of functioning or need.

Superimposed upon differences that are due to degree of severity of the visual impairment, there are equally significant ones that are associated with chronological age and with age of onset of the impairment. These factors serve to sub-divide an already small client population into even smaller groupings. According to the Department of Health (DOH, 1991), the number of people on the registers of the blind in England in 1991 was 136,195, an increase of 26 per cent over the period 1980–91. Among these registered as partially sighted, the percentage increase is even greater, the rise from 51,426 to 93,777 being of the order of 82 per cent. As Tables 1.1 and 1.2 show, the overall increases are due almost entirely to the rise in the numbers of people aged 75 years and above. It is clear, therefore, that most of these people are not congenitally blind; their impairment is due to the ageing processes of physical and sensory deterioration.

Table 1.1 Number of people on the register of the blind, by age. England 1980–91. (Derived from Department of Health, Personal Social Services, Local Authority Statistics, Ref: A/F7)

As at 31 March	0–4	5–15	16–49	50–64	65–74	75+	Age unknown	Total
1980	254	1,781	10,993	13,637	19,499	61,349	252	107,765
1981	..	..	..	..	..	..	..	..
1982	275	1,709	11,471	13,422	19,376	65,476	0	111,729
1983–5	..	..	..	..	..	..	..	..
1986	378	1,519	12,508	12,783	18,982	74,378	0	120,548
1987	..	..	..	..	..	..	..	..
1988	452	1,595	12,894	12,518	19,521	79,848	0	126,828
1989–90	..	..	..	..	..	..	..	..
1991	668	1,886	13,772	11,876	18,658	89,335	0	136,195

.. Data not available

3

Table 1.2 Number of people on the register of the partially sighted, by age. England 1980−91. (Derived from Department of Health, Personal Social Services, Local Authority Statistics, Ref: A/F7)

As at 31 March	0−4	5−15	16−49	50−64	65−74	75+	Age unknown	Total
				Number of persons aged:				
1980	157	2,226	7,964	5,172	8,494	27,292	121	51,426
1981	..	..	..	..	..	..	..	..
1982	165	2,062	8,662	5,635	9,417	32,062	0	58,003
1983−5	..	..	..	..	..	..	..	..
1986	177	1,768	9,731	6,282	10,994	45,152	0	71,104
1987	..	..	..	..	..	..	..	..
1988	215	1,679	10,304	6,755	11,792	48,303	0	79,048
1989−90	..	..	..	..	..	..	..	..
1991	366	1,778	11,161	7,593	13,284	59,595	0	93,777

.. Data not available

The Department of Health issues warnings as to the accuracy and reliability of its triennial statistics, and some idea of the uncertainty about the real size of the population can be gleaned from the RNIB survey of blind and partially sighted adults in the whole of Britain (Bruce et al., 1991): that report suggests that there are roughly three times as many blind and partially sighted people as previously estimated, the total number probably being almost one million.

Classificatory factors

Before any assessment of a visually handicapped person is carried out to measure particular skills and levels of achievement, it is essential that the assessor should record information about the client's chronological age, the age of onset of the visual impairment, and the degree and extent of any remaining vision. A failure to take these factors into account can

4

lead to the selection of inappropriate testing procedures and to consequential failure to obtain as comprehensive an understanding as possible of current attainments. Conversely, knowledge about these variables may serve to enhance the tester's insight into what the client has had to overcome to reach his present status. At the purely technical level, knowledge about them is important for establishing rapport with the client. In attempting to demonstrate some of the specific reasons for gathering information of this nature, it is also the intention to argue that the assessor has a responsibility to discover it herself rather than relying solely upon that recorded in any other formal reports prepared by colleagues in the medical and related professions.

Chronological age

For the assessor, chronological age is significant, whether or not there is any sensory impairment. It affects decisions as to which tests to use, how to administer them and how to interpret the results. More specifically:

(1) It gives rise to expectations about what can and cannot be tackled. This is especially the case in relation to what are labelled as 'information' items in intelligence and achievement tests. For example, knowledge of a child's age will influence expectations of how he will cope with the verbal comprehension, verbal fluency, word definition, and similarities sub-scales of the British Ability Scales and with comparable parts of the Williams Intelligence Test for Children with Defective Vision. Indeed, the subject's chronological age will often act as a guide as to which item in a test should be the starting point. This is true of nearly all tests that are designed for individual, as opposed to group, administration and is of considerable importance in tests that cover a wide age range, such as the British Picture Vocabulary Scale (Dunn *et al.*, 1982), which can be informative to an experienced assessor about a subject's visual perception skills, although it was constructed as a measure of receptive vocabulary. Many tests are, of course, designed within a developmental framework or model. The notion of 'development' is inextricably linked to chronological age, with the latter being used as one of its major indices.

(2) The validity and reliability of some categories of tests are affected by the subject's age and maturity. This is especially so in relation to personality assessment. With young visually handicapped children, the low reliability of the available measures — however valid they may be — casts doubt upon their usefulness. (As will be seen, their use with older subjects is made problematical, since the

process of adjusting to the diagnosis and to the onset of the visual disability is not well understood, either in terms of its effects upon personality or in terms of the length of time required for adjustment to the impairment and its personal and social consequences.) Age can therefore be an indicator of how informative a test is likely to be.

(3) The subject's expectations as to the purpose of the assessment and its outcome are intimately linked to his age. Fourteen year olds being assessed for school/college placement or pre-vocational training courses will have an understanding about the importance of the assessment that will not be the same as that of eight year olds being assessed for 'statementing' purposes. Blind adults will have hopes and anxieties of a very different nature when they are confronted with a battery of test procedures that may affect their vocational ambitions. These different perceptions are age related to a large extent, and should influence the assessor's choice of instrument, her explanation of its nature and her mode of administering it.

(4) Closely related to this last point is the influence that the subject's age can have upon the nature of the relationship between assessor and subject. Although objectivity is one of the basic requirements in any situation involving appraisal of another person, it cannot be regarded as some kind of unchanging approach, a cloak that can be donned to signify who is the assessor and who the subject. It depends, rather, upon putting the subject at his ease and creating circumstances in which he can operate at his optimal level. A good assessor will therefore behave differently with different subjects, and one of the factors that will determine this behaviour is the age of the client. An adult assessor with a congenitally blind six year old will find it necessary to send different signals from those she would send to an adult; indeed, the goal of objectivity will demand a different approach to an age contemporary than to an older adult. These differences will manifest themselves in the style of language to be used and in the degree of familiarity and formality between the two participants.

Age of onset

We still know relatively little about how congenitally blind children develop concepts of objects and events in a world which they have never seen. What we do know is that sighted children, before the age of five, have already learned an enormous amount about the world in which they live. Much, probably most, of this learning has been done casually, informally, without the direct and directed supervision or help of their adult care-givers. Much, again probably most, of this learning has been mediated through vision.

It is generally agreed that very early onset of blindness, especially at or before birth, has effects on 'motor development'. People with extensive experience claim to be able to tell in most cases whether blind five year olds were blind from birth, merely by observing the way they walk and run. Many blind infants have to be taught how to sit, how to crawl and how to walk. All too often, there is a disinclination to move from the prone, the supine and the sitting positions. Ensuing poor posture, awkward gait and body control (including rocking) often persist into later childhood, and even into adolescence and adult life.

Why should this be? In broad terms, it can be attributed to (a) a lack of visual stimuli, visual incentives, that draw the child outwards to reach for and explore his immediate physical world; (b) the lack of 'feedback' about what the world consists of and about the 'rewards' that come from manipulating and controlling that world; and (c) the absence of the ability to imitate (by the mere act of looking at) the movements and gestures of adults and other children more developmentally advanced than themselves.

Having had sight for a couple of years enables children who become blind in early childhood to stand and walk 'better' than the congenitally blind for some time. It seems to affect the way they hold themselves and the way they orient their bodies to other people. This, in turn, affects the way other people regard them and interact with them.

In so far as we do know anything about the ways in which concepts are acquired and elaborated by sighted children, we recognize firstly, the importance of their having a sufficient quantity of experiences and practice with the concepts, and secondly, the importance of having opportunities to perceive exemplars that differ in some way from the first examples of the concept. To take a particular instance: the child acquires the concept (and the verbal label) 'chair' mainly through direct experience of a particular chair and hearing the name given to it; after repeated exposures, he becomes familiar with that chair and the label, the word, attached to it. By virtue of his sense of vision, he also sees many other things that have a lot in common with his CHAIR. But they differ somewhat in shape, colour, texture, height, width, depth, weight, etc. His sense of vision provides him, quite fortuitously, with all these casual experiences, and he proceeds to generalize the concept of chair to all these other, perceptually dissimilar, objects. For the blind child, this facility to generalize and to transfer is not so readily available.

The blind child who has been sighted for a few years has been exposed to the world, and the objects and events in it, in an entirely 'richer' way than his congenitally blind brother or sister. It has been borne in upon him, with little direct input from other human beings, how the three-dimensional world is organized and how it seems to change as he moves around inside it. Things are constantly changing; and yet in some very important respects they do not change. And these invariances – these qualities that endure across apparent physical change – are aspects of his world and his life that enable him to undergo new learning experiences. They help him to impose an orderliness upon the world, and thus provide him with a framework of understanding that is not so readily available to the congenitally blind child.

When we come to carry out any kind of perceptual, social and cognitive assessment of the blind and severely visually impaired child, we must be prepared to recognize our ignorance of the world as he has experienced it. We must be alert to cues that might show us where there are gaps in his experience. There will not be the raising of eyebrows, the widening of the eyes and those other tell-tale signs that show that a sighted child has misunderstood or not understood the question. For the blind child who has never seen, the intelligence test items that present what the assessor may consider to be commonplace examples of commonplace concrete objects, may be totally incomprehensible because the objects are of a size, a feel and a weight that are quite unfamiliar to the child.

Age of onset should be thought of, then, both as a potentially invisible barrier that may have shut the child off from certain valuable kinds of experience and that may shut off the assessors from any awareness of their – and the child's – ignorance; and, especially for the adult blinded in middle life, as a determining variable, changing over time as acceptance and adjustment proceed.

Residual vision

The significance of the amount of residual vision still retained cannot be over-emphasized. Failure to take it into account before embarking on assessment of other kinds of functioning can result in the choice of inappropriate measuring procedures and in very gross mis-measurement of the cognitive, perceptual, motor and social skills that may be the particular concern of the assessor.

For those who are totally blind, or have perception of light and dark, or can only detect large objects, or can do no more than 'count fingers' at close range, then all procedures that rely upon visual presentation of the test items will, of course, be inappropriate. This precludes, therefore, all visually presented tests of reading accuracy, reading speed and reading comprehension. These visual limitations will also debar the use of tests of intelligence, aptitude, personality, attitudes and achievement, the instructions for which are presented in print and to which a written response is required.

Like age of onset, the amount of residual vision will indicate what is likely to be known about the 'visual world' and thus affects the spoken instructions that are used in the testing. For example:

'Look at these pictures' (as in the British Picture Vocabulary Scale);
'Make a pattern of beads like this one' (as in the Williams Test);
'Which of these would you rather be or do' (as in a personality test).

The extent to which a child is prepared to use his residual vision may tell us something about his level of intelligence, about the nature of the family's support and their attitude to his visual disability, and about the opportunities for learning that are already available.

For adventitiously blinded adults, especially those who have finished their formal education and have had a wide-ranging experience of the worlds of work and leisure before the onset of the disability, the process of adjusting to total blindness or severe visual disability presents a very different set of problems. While assessment should take account of skills and knowledge acquired before the onset of the impairment (with no undue avoidance of 'visually' based instructions such as 'Look at this'), it must also be informed by an awareness not only of the emotional consequences of recently acquired blindness but also of the attendant slowness and uncertainty in carrying out tasks that require reliance upon touch rather than vision. The congenitally blind adult will probably not display the same degree of uncertainty in such circumstances and it is likely that he will be more skilled in listening to oral instructions. The experienced tester will therefore not hesitate to ask about the duration of the disability and to ensure that instructions are repeated as necessary.

With adults, knowledge about the quality and effectiveness of any remaining sight will be used to decide whether the test should be presented in visual or tactual format (where such alternatives may exist). In general, it is advisable to allow the subject to make the final decision. The purpose, after all, is to elicit the highest level of achievement of which he is capable so that the results of the testing can be used to enable him to make a judgement about further training or job selection. There is, nevertheless, much to be said for presenting parallel visual and tactile versions since differential performance can be informative to the assessor and the adult subject himself.

CHAPTER 2

Assessing Residual Vision and Visual Perception

Formal and clinical methods of assessing residual vision

In most cases, teachers and rehabilitation professionals will meet their clients, whether child or adult, after formal, ophthalmic assessment of vision has been completed and after 'registration' has occurred. The information obtained from the ophthalmic reports will certainly need supplementing, for teaching and programme-planning purposes, by direct and prolonged observation of visual competence over a wide range of work, study and leisure activities. As will be argued in due course, informal and non-standardized methods of assessment can be very informative, and not merely as a means of cross-checking on what has been revealed by the objective methods of the ophthalmologists and optometrists. Nevertheless, it is the eye-specialists' diagnosis of visual impairment and their measurement of visual functioning that constitute the starting point of the rehabilitation worker's involvement with her client, and as a member of a multi-disciplinary team she must be familiar with the major areas of concern of her ophthalmic colleagues. This does not necessitate knowledge about the pathology of the globe and the visual pathways to the brain, but it does pre-suppose some understanding of distant and near-vision acuity, visual fields, colour vision and contrast sensitivity because these are among the most important factors that can influence the client's ability to carry out his day-to-day activities. The clinical measurement of these parameters and the detailed interpretation of the results are the responsibility of the eye-specialist; the test instruments and procedures are normally available for use only by ophthalmologists, optometrists and vision scientists.

Visual acuity

Visual acuity refers to the ability to detect, make discriminations among, and recognize objects and events in the visual field. For adults, the most commonly used test of distance vision is the Snellen Chart, which consists of rows of symbols varying in size. Typically, the symbol in the top row is of such a size that the angle it subtends on the retina, when viewed from a distance of 6 metres in the clinic, corresponds to the physical size of a letter that can be read at a distance of 60 metres by people with normal sight. The lower rows on the Chart present symbols decreasing in size, and such that they can be recognized by a normally sighted person at 36 metres, 24 metres and down to 6 metres or nearer. The ensuing measurement is expressed as an index such as 6/18, indicating that the reader sees at 6 metres a symbol that is discernible by most people at 18 metres. Each eye is tested separately, and then both eyes together, the reported indices being those calculated after optimal correction with the aid of lenses.

There are many alternative chart-based tests of distance vision especially for use with children. One, known as the E Chart, requires a child who is a non-reader to turn a cut-out letter E so that it is pointing in the same direction as the symbols (all in the shape of an E) printed on the chart. The printed symbols vary in size, as with the conventional Snellen Chart, and the same numerical indices of distance acuity are obtainable. The maximum reliability of these tests is achieved when administered by qualified, experienced eye-specialists in clinical settings where levels of luminance and other factors can be held constant. Results obtained under other conditions, as in a classroom or office, are much less reliable, but this may be of practical significance for the client and his adviser since it may point to the difficulties he may be confronting in the real-life world of the workplace or classroom.

This notion of the context is also embedded in near-vision tests, which are typically administered at 'reading distance', thus acknowledging the fact that visual acuity is complex and not amenable to summary in a single index. A frequently used test of near-vision is the 'N' point test, consisting of cards on which letter symbols of different sizes are printed. The results are reported in terms of the smallest print size (e.g. N12 or N16) that can be read, either at a normal reading distance of 14 inches or at the subject's preferred distance. For children, the Sheridan–Gardiner materials (Sheridan and Gardiner, 1970) were designed as a portable vision-screening test 'applicable under school conditions and suitable for the assessment of distant and near-vision'.

There are obvious advantages in a single procedure that allows both sorts of acuity to be tested and that makes it possible 'to discover the child's everyday visual capacity at home, in the street, and in the classroom' (ibid.). As with so many of the chart and card-based procedures, however, it does not measure the very low acuities found among children registrable as blind (below 6/60 Snellen), and yet many of these pupils can, given good lighting and other conditions, learn to make sense of what is present in their visual field, including the deciphering of text and print diagrams. An alternative and more up-to-date test of distant and near-vision that can be used with adults and with children from about 2.5 years of age is the Sonksen Silver Acuity System (available from Messrs Keller Ltd.). Testing is done for distance vision at 3 or 6 metres, and the 'flip-over' cards make administration quick and simple. The Sonksen Picture Guide to Visual Function (Sonksen and Macrae, 1987) recognizes that simple acuity measures do not bring out the difficulties that a child may have in coping with the complex, coloured pictures that are to be found in nursery and infant classrooms; this, therefore, is another useful test for assessing the kind of functional vision that is relevant in real life, as opposed to purely clinical situations.

A further distinction has to be made between measures of acuity in which single symbols are presented and those where there is a whole line or group of letters, numbers or pictures. The former may give rise to higher 'scores' by a very young child, with Hyvarinen and Lindstedt (1981) stating that a 'child may have a 2−3 times better visual acuity for single symbols than for symbols in line'. This so-called 'visual crowding' phenomenon has been investigated by Atkinson and her colleagues at the University of Cambridge's Visual Development Unit. Good, single-symbol acuity may lead to higher expectations of a pupil's ability to cope with traditional pre-reading and beginning-reading schemes, and for this reason the Cambridge Crowding Cards acuity test (as published by Clement Clarke International) can provide useful, diagnostic information for teachers of severely visually impaired children.

Visual fields

The field of vision is the area which can be seen without any movement of the eye or head. Objects within this area can be seen simultaneously, but those on the periphery will not be seen with any great clarity or sharpness; movement of the eye will normally bring such objects into sharp focus. In some diseases of the eye, parts of the visual field may be non-functional; defects on the periphery can affect mobility, while a central scotoma (a blind or partially blind spot) will cause difficulties with reading and other tasks requiring the detection of fine detail. The clinician has methods for plotting the shape and size of the visual field with great precision and for assessing the effects of varying brightness of objects within the field. Devices such as kampimeters, perimeters and visual field analysers are used for these purposes; the teacher and rehabilitation worker will need the eye-specialist to report and interpret the results of such tests. Even the peripheral field testing in the STYCAR Vision Test (Sheridan, 1976) requires considerable experience, and help from an assistant, to ensure valid findings with the young children for whom it is designed. The 'confrontation' or Donders procedure is a simple, if somewhat subjective and imprecise, method that can be employed with adults and older children. Tester and subject face each other, fixating their gaze upon the other's eyes, and the subject reports when he detects the tester's finger as it is moved inwards from various parts of the periphery. The inexactness and low reliability of this method places it more properly among the informal, observational techniques discussed below, but the experienced tester can certainly glean from it some understanding of the kind of difficulty the client may have in workaday situations requiring the registration of objects and people outside the central area of gaze.

Colour vision

For an adult or an adolescent concerned with vocational choices, colour blindness can be a major handicap, even if it is accepted that the 'clinical and practical significance of uncomplicated colour deficiency in a healthy child is not very great' (Hyvarinen and Lindstedt, 1981, p.40). For the severely visually impaired child, account has to be taken of the modern emphasis in special schools in encouraging the maximum use of any residual vision, however slight. Barraga's work (e.g. Barraga, 1970) and the *Look and Think* project (Tobin *et al.*, 1979; revised edition, Chapman *et al.*, 1989) point to the benefits of early, regular and structured training for developing the necessary perceptual and cognitive skills that make it possible to extract information from two- and three-dimensional arrays. Failure to note colour-vision defects and to select appropriate colour alternatives can render parts of these training programmes ineffective.

Among the many tests used for assessing colour vision, the quickest to administer are the pseudoisochromatic charts, of which the Ishihara plates are an example. The plates are made up of patterns of coloured dots in which are embedded the shapes of numerals, themselves made up of variously coloured dots. It has been argued (e.g. Hyvarinen and Lindstedt, 1981) that these 'confusion' tests of colour blindness, despite their ease of use, are rather too sensitive for children, 'giving many false-positives' (ibid., p.41); that is, colour blindness is being identified when it is in fact absent, the child's failure to do the task correctly being due to other factors, e.g. misunderstanding of what is being asked.

Another test designed for use with children is the City University Colour Vision Test (Fletcher, 1980) which requires the child to match a centrally placed coloured dot with its counterpart located among others on the periphery of the card.

Other colour tests used by clinicians involve the matching of colours, the sorting of coloured caps into a progression based upon hue and the mixing of colours to achieve equality with a master or standard. More sophisticated techniques present the stimuli by means of lanterns that allow variation of size (and apparent distance) and luminosity, and are thus useful for vocational-testing purposes. With the severely visually impaired child or adult, the accurate appraisal of colour vision will be beyond the resource of all but the highly trained eye-specialist who can keep control of all the other significant factors. For example, differences in brightness of the test objects can lead to the failure to detect some colour-vision defects.

Contrast sensitivity

'Luminance' is a measure of the amount of light emitted by a surface, and contrast sensitivity is the term applied to the eye's ability to register differences in the luminance of objects, whether two- or three-dimensionally presented. In some books the luminance differences between 'figure' and 'ground' are so small that they are difficult to detect by people with central visual acuities below 3/60 Snellen. At higher levels of acuity, the detection of contrast may also be restricted and this is one of the reasons that informal assessment of low levels of visual acuity may be so unreliable. It is not possible for contrast sensitivity to be measured other than by sophisticated techniques, and yet the practitioner interested in encouraging and developing the optimal use of residual vision must be alert to the possibility that poor visual functioning is due not merely to low acuity, defective colour vision, restricted visual fields or low intelligence. Closed circuit television (CCTV) devices and micro-computer visual display units (VDUs) can improve contrast differences among the elements of an array, and the practitioner may gain some indication that contrast sensitivity needs formal examining by observation of apparent differences in performance as between conventional book/paper presentation of text and CCTV or VDU presentation of the same materials. The clinician and vision scientist may then explore contrast thresholds and contrast sensitivity by such means as sinusoidal grading procedures, the most sophisticated of which allow them to vary the illumination, the size of the stimulus, the space between stimuli and the duration of the exposure.

Assessing visual perception skills in children

Perception, the ability to make sense of the stimuli falling on the retina, is not merely a function of the health and efficiency of the various parts of the globe and the visual system. Interpreting the visual stimuli transmitted to the brain requires that they be associated with other sensory data and with previously received, interpreted, coded and stored information. Making these associations is a skill that develops throughout childhood, and is therefore dependent upon the quality and quantity of experience and of the learning opportunities available to the child. The adventitiously visually impaired adult brings to the task of interpreting what he sees a range of knowledge, skills and decoding strategies not yet acquired by the congenitally impaired child with the same objectively measured levels of visual acuity. Some notion of this can be gained by presenting such a child and such an adult with a visual array (two or three dimensional) and asking them to describe what they see. The adult will typically scan the whole scene, suspending his judgement until he can place objects and events into relationship with one another. One of the results of this 'viewing the whole scene' is that more is seen or, rather, more appears to be seen. Objects that are partly occluded by others are identified, not because of superior acuity, visual field or colour sense but on account of where they are located in relation to other objects. His scanning will be systematic and purposive. The young child on the other hand will tend to focus on whatever is first seen or may move his gaze from one element to another in a haphazard fashion, and he thus is unable to use the 'whole' to help him decipher individual, ambiguous parts of the array. The child will also not have the same internal 'dictionary' against which the new data can be compared. With growth in experience will come greater facility and speed in recognizing what is displayed. For the parent and teacher, an essential task will be to provide the structured experience that will enable the young visually impaired child to acquire the perceptual and cognitive competence that his fully sighted peer will acquire in a relatively unstructured manner.

In so far as each child's experience is highly individualized, it is impossible to devise standardized procedures for comprehensively assessing the visual perceptual competence of, for example, all severely visually impaired five year olds. Nevertheless, there are sub-sets of this competence that are highly relevant to the kinds of tasks that such children encounter on entry to school, and the fact that scores or other numerical indices cannot be derived from these methods of assessment is not a major drawback. The claim is that these methods measure something over and above sensory acuity, and its substantiation is to be found in the experienced teacher's appraisal of the information and in the way in which she then uses it for remediating the under-developed skills.

There are now two instruments that can be used for this purpose. The first of them, the Barraga Visual Efficiency Scale (Barraga, 1964; 1970), contains 4 sub-scales designed to evaluate the child's ability to respond – usually on a matching-to-sample basis – to items of increasing complexity in size, detail and interpretation. The first section consists of 12 items

> related to the discrimination and matching of geometric form, object contour, light-dark intensity, and size and position in space. Section 2 requires the discrimination and matching of figure size, object and abstract figure detail, position of figures in space and image constancy of outlines, pattern details and objects. The third . . . presents items for visual closure of figures, spatial perspective of figure outlines . . . [and the fourth] requires the discrimination of size, position, sequence and relationship of letter and word symbols. (Barraga, 1970)

Although the scale only contains items presented in two-dimensional format, the associated teaching activities and materials for the development of visual perceptual abilities comprise two- and three-dimensional objects.

Within the United States, investigations have been carried out to assess the validity and reliability of the test (e.g. Harley and Spollen, 1973; Harley *et al.*, 1973). In this country, Tobin (1972) examined the effectiveness of the suggested teaching procedures for children registered as blind, and Foster (1973) described an investigation 'designed to observe the VES in operation with partially sighted children, and with sighted children who were to act as a baseline for comparison'. One consequence of Foster's study is a recommended revised set of instructions for administering the scale to British children. The 48 items that make up the test can be presented quickly and easily, no verbal responses being called for from the child, and constitute an efficient method of obtaining information about the visual discriminations the child can make, particularly in relation to tasks relevant to classroom learning.

The second instrument, the 'Look and Think Checklist' (Tobin *et al.*, 1979; revised edition, Chapman *et al.*, 1989), is an extension of the Barraga Visual Efficiency Scale and was devised quite specifically for use by teachers of the visually handicapped. The age range of the children with whom the assessment procedures and associated remedial teaching materials were validated was five to eleven years but it is now also being used with even younger children. The authors deliberately eschew the use of the word 'test', although they do point out that the Checklist was subjected to the kinds of empirical testing and statistical analysis normally associated with the construction and validation of standardized achievement and aptitude tests. It does not give rise to a standardized score or a perceptual quotient, nor even a visual perception age. It is described as an

> instrument for the orderly and structured observation of a child's present level of functioning in specified visual skills . . . [and] is an inventory for recording those areas in which it becomes evident to the teacher that improvement can take place if the appropriate stimulation and practice are provided. The Checklist can, therefore, only be as efficient as the teacher who uses and interprets it. (ibid., p.6)

As can be seen in Figure 2.1, the results of the assessment are recorded on a 'Summary and Profile Sheet', the final three columns of which permit the construction of a 'profile' of the child's strengths and weaknesses. The 18 units of the Checklist cover aspects of the traditional areas of object, form and outline, space, movement, and colour perception. The arrangement of the units takes account of ease of administration, with four units consisting of concrete objects (full-size and model) preceding a further nine units involving various kinds of two-dimensional representations; there are then three units in which the child or the teacher acts or draws, and the list is concluded with two units to do with colour discrimination and naming.

18

Figure 2.1 Imaginary summary and profile sheet for 'Look and Think' Checklist

SKILL	SCORE GRADING			PROFILE				
	Under Development	Partially Developed	Developed	Under development	Developed	Partially	Developed	Developed
1. Naming: 3-D Objects	0 1 2	3 4	**5** 6					X
2. Naming: 3-D Models	0 1 2	3 4	5 **6**					X
3. Discrimination: 3-D	0 1 2	3 4	**5** 6					X
4. Matching: 3-D	0 1 2	3 4	**5** 6					X
5. Matching: 2-D	0 1 2 3	4 5 **6**	7 8				X	
6. Simple Perspective: 2-D	0 1 2	3 4	**5**					X
7. Using Critical Features: Exploded Drawings	0 1	**2** 3	4				X	
8. Naming and Describing: Photographs	0 1 2	3 4	**5**					X
9. Naming and Describing: Drawings	0 1 2	3 4 5	**7** 8					X
10. Perception of Symmetry	0 1 **2**	3 4	5		X			
11. Perception of Patterns	0 1 **2**	3 4	5		X			
12. Classifying Facial Expressions: Photographs	0 1 **2** 3	4 5 6 7 8 9	10 11 12		X			
13. Identification from Body Postures: Drawings	0 1 2	3 4	**5**					X
14. Perception of Gestures and Body Movement	0 1	2 3	**4**					X
15. Hand-eye Co-ordination: Paper and Pencil Maze								
A	46 upwards	36–45 secs.	**35** secs. and lower					X
B	51 upwards	46–50 secs.	**45** secs. and lower					X
16. Hand-eye Co-ordination: Magnet Board	0 1	2 3 4	*5* upwards					X
17. Colour Differentiation	0 1 2	3 4 5 6	**7**					X
18. Colour Naming	0 1 2	3 4 5	**6**					X

Apart from the information derived from the raw scores on the various units of the Checklist, the authors claim that the experienced teacher can use the child's responses to discover something about:

(i) his pre-school experience with three-dimensional objects and two-dimensional forms of presentation;

(ii) his facility with relational concepts referred to by expressions such as 'different from', 'bigger than', 'nearer than', 'higher than', etc.;

(iii) the distance at which he is able to, or prefers to, view his work;

(iv) the visual discriminations he can make in the kinds of activities commonly undertaken in the classroom;

(v) the comprehensiveness of his search and scan activities and his willingness to delay judgement until enough visual information has been gathered and evaluated;

(vi) his general attention span;

(vii) the time he needs to complete various simple and complex tasks requiring visual monitoring and checking.

It will be apparent that these procedures are motivated by a belief that assessment should and can be used as the pre-cursor of remedial or developmental programmes to enable the child to move on. Between them they cover the full age range from birth to eleven years of age, and both their real and superficial differences cannot disguise the fact that the tests are also often tapping similar competencies – involving language, reasoning, discriminating and memory. While it must not be inferred that they can be used as substitutes, they can help to cross-validate one another in certain areas of functioning; their differences in content and general orientation (for example, mental as against perceptual) can then be seen as filling and rounding out our understanding of the child's abilities.

Informal methods: introduction

The measurement and description of vision presented in the medical reports that are used for 'registration' purposes can be of only limited value to the rehabilitation officer, the psychologist, the peripatetic adviser and the teacher in the classroom. This is due in part to the fact that these statements are primarily medical and legal in form and function. That is, they are formulated for passing on information among medical practitioners and for establishing, for social services personnel, whether the client is to be classified as blind or partially sighted, and thus possibly eligible for certain statutory entitlements. They are not formulated to enable the various non-medical professionals to ascertain what can be perceived and how much can be perceived in the ordinary environment of the home, the workplace, the classroom and the street. The reports do not, either, say very much about the 'dynamics' of seeing and perceiving; they do not, in other words, provide information about what the client can use his vision for under different lighting conditions, at different distances and in relation to different tasks (e.g. crossing the road, watching a television, reading a book or a computer screen, using a pen or a typewriter keyboard, or playing sports and games). These forms were not designed for these purposes. The assessment of a client's 'functional' vision must therefore be accepted as a responsibility by the non-medical professionals if they are to be of assistance to him during the course of his education or rehabilitation.

As already discussed, when the ophthalmologist and ophthalmic optician measure vision, one essential requirement is that they use standardized, objective procedures. Their aim is to obtain valid and reliable scores, summarizing the client's visual acuity and visual fields in terms of numerical indices. In order to do this, optimal levels of lighting must be provided in the clinical setting, and the measurements must be made at specified distances. These conditions do not hold, however, in the home, the workplace and the classroom. In these situations, what is needed is a 'profile' of the client's visual functioning in relation to the various tasks and activities that are part of his everyday life. At present, there are no properly standardized, and therefore reliable, methods for eliciting this kind of information, and the practitioner must use informal procedures. These procedures also have the great merit that they can simultaneously combine teaching and testing, a practice that is inherent in the very roles of teachers, parents and rehabilitation professionals.

Even in the course of an initial and brief meeting with a client, whether child or adult, something can be gleaned about his ability and willingness to use any remaining sight. Posture, gait and hand—eye co-ordination can all provide useful information to the practised observer. The angle at which the body and head are held when the client is seated may indicate whether one eye is better than another and whether there is a preferred distance for examining books or other objects offered to him. How he moves in the familiar environment of the kitchen, office, classroom or workshop can bring out how well he can pick up cues at an intermediate distance. The fluency of movements involved in locating and using pens, cutlery and tools will be indicative of how well the eyes are able to monitor and provide feedback to him.

The actual process of teaching an adult how to organize an office, workstation or kitchen in order to optimize the visual conditions will offer numerous opportunities for informally assessing functional vision. The height, brightness and colour of equipment and utensils — and of the walls and surfaces against which they are set — can be important factors in making them easily discernible. In working with her client to make the right selections, the rehabilitation officer can use this teaching situation to make judgements of an immediately applicable nature about near and intermediate visual acuities, extent of visual field, colour vision and the effects of varying the placement and the required power of lamps and other lighting fitments. In teaching a newly registered person the best route to the local shops and post office, the instructor will be able to observe whether fixed landmarks can be noticed — advertising hoardings, belisha beacons, traffic lights — and whether functional vision appears to vary owing to changes in levels of lighting on entry to and departure from shopping arcades and other enclosed areas. Changes in competence may be misleading if account is not taken of the possible effects of non-visual stimuli, such as sounds (of traffic, children playing, workmen) and smells (from butchers' and fruiterers' shops). These non-visual cues can seem to enhance or interfere with the client's use of his sight; a distinction needs to be made between the information he is getting through his eyes and what he is registering and using from the combined and dynamic use of all his sensory organs. The varied teaching situations available to the instructor will not provide numerical indices summarizing visual acuities and fields, but they can be seen as means of cross-checking the validity of inferences drawn about the performance in a given situation, and the fact that performance seems to vary as information becomes available through the other sensory modalities will be something that both instructor and client can use to improve levels of functioning even further.

Informal methods: children

With a very young child, especially one below about two-and-a-half years of age, some indication of basic functioning can be obtained by observing whether he will fixate his attention on a small torch light or a brightly coloured object that is held before him centrally and at head height while he is in a seated position. By varying the size, distance and brightness of the stimulus and noting whether he follows it as it is moved from side to side and up and down, the tester will derive some information of practical importance about the child's visual acuity in his normal environment. Where there are positive responses to these stimuli, and if the infant is still alert, his preferential looking behaviour can be examined by presentation of two- and three-dimensional objects. Although formal assessment requires special apparatus and training, some general understanding can be obtained about the major variables, e.g. size, distance, movement, brightness, complexity and contrast, which may influence the child's preferences. In the first few months of life, a preference is shown for bright, high contrast, simple shapes, particularly when presented in two-dimensional, i.e. pictorial, format. As the child grows, more complex shapes tend to be fixated in preference to simpler ones, and lower levels of contrast can be dealt with. The immediate practical purpose of assessing informally in the home is to enable parents to provide lighting and toys that will encourage the infant to use his residual vision and thus learn something about his world. With older children of pre-school age, preferential looking can be used as a means of developing language skills involving relational terms such as 'bigger than', 'farther away', 'as bright as', etc. Conversely, for the child who is already proficient in such skills, the words can be used to direct his attention so that he is encouraged to look for finer visual distinctions among objects and events in the near and mid-distance environment of the classroom and the home.

Among children of school age, the ability to resolve – make discriminations among – visually presented objects can be influenced by the proximity of other objects. Satisfactory performance on tasks in which only one printed symbol is to be recognized may not be perfectly correlated with achievement on tasks where letters are grouped closely together, as in words and sentences. The 'crowding effect' may be such as to make it difficult or impossible for the young reader to interpret letter shapes and sizes that are well within his range of competence when presented singly. Even in the busy, non-standardized conditions of the classroom, it is possible for the teacher with a young reader, known to have a visual disability, to do some informal assessment of this phenomenon. Once the child has learned to recognize and name individual letter shapes and pick out individual words, they can be written out to form two or three lines. Comparison of accuracy and speed of performance between single, well-spaced-out letter arrays and the continuous letter and word strings may show whether a formal examination by an ophthalmic optician should be asked for; an obvious deterioration in performance will at least alert parent and teacher to the possibility that poor reading is associated with the visual disability rather than with any cognitive disability. In keeping with the testing-through-teaching philosophy, parents and teachers can vary the letter size, the lighting, and the distance and angle at which the book is held, and thus build up a picture of the child's needs and preferences when reading and writing. With these observations to hand, discussions with the ophthalmic optician during formal testing can be more informative, with advice being sought as to the optimal conditions for reading and as to the kinds of low vision aids suited to these conditions.

As the RNIB survey (Walker *et al.*, 1992) has revealed, some 56 per cent of visually impaired children have at least one other disability. In principle, the same informal methods of assessing residual vision and visual perceptual skills can be used with these multi-handicapped children. However, even lower levels of functioning may have to be looked for. Simple reaction to light of varying intensity and colour can be noted in the playroom and classroom, even if some of the reactions are of an aversive nature (covering the eyes with their hands or turning the head away) or of an obsessive or addictive nature (prolonged gazing at light from electric torches). Simple visual tracking of a light, a toy or a household utensil can be monitored by teachers and parents in the ordinary course of play. Does he try to maintain eye contact during games and does he reach out to objects as they are brought towards him? It is certainly possible to develop some notion of his visual capacities, upwards from the mere sensation of light, to non-tactual recognition of familiar objects, to visuo-motor skills and to complex visual perception, the latter being demonstrated by the correct use and positioning of cutlery and cups, by building tower blocks, by matching colours and shapes, by visual sequencing and by visual memory. The immediate purpose of such informal assessment is the design of play and object-manipulation exercises that will serve to increase his understanding of the nature of his world and his ability to use and control it.

Informal methods: adults

With adults, especially those who are newly registered as blind or partially sighted, the most straightforward approach is to ask them what they can see, and if this enquiry is set in the context of discussing with them what their ambitions are and what assistance they would like, then it will be seen as neither insensitive nor idle curiosity. Questions about what can be seen in the room will be indicative of the kind of training that may be required in the general area of daily living skills − cooking, cleaning, hygiene, indoor mobility − and also show what aids and modifications to the home may be useful. The location and intensity of lights, the colour of utensils, the contrast between utensils and the surfaces on which they are placed, hung and used, and the lay-out of offices and other workplaces can facilitate or interfere with a client's ability to operate efficiently. Questions about what can be seen recognize the client's own role in designing an optimal environment for him.

They may, however, not be sufficient since to begin with the newly blinded person may not know what can be done, or not be consciously aware of what he can see. In conjunction with direct questioning, the assessor can use a variety of simple observational procedures to round out her understanding of the usefulness of any remaining sight. For example, does there seem to be a preferred angle — inferred from head and body posture — at which objects and people are observed? Is there evidence of visual monitoring of arm and hand movements when cups, glasses and tools are being reached for? How quickly are movements detected when objects are brought into the visual field? Are such detections poorer when objects and movements occur in one particular part of the visual field (to the left, right, above and below)? Can any kind of print size still be deciphered (for example, newspaper headlines and names of substances on food packaging)? Are obstacles, such as furniture and workplace equipment, avoided as the client moves around in familiar places? When coupled with the answers to direct questioning, this informal observation can confirm, expand or call into question the information obtained from the formal, ophthalmic testing; it can then form the basis of the assessor's recommendations to her client as to what other assessment procedures might be useful and as to what changes in his environment and in his everyday behaviour might bring about significant gains in functioning.

CHAPTER 3

Pre-school Blind and Partially Sighted Children

Purposes and underlying assumptions

In *Warnock's Eighteen Per Cent*, Gipps, Gross and Goldstein (1987) discuss the reasons currently given for testing whole groups of young children. Three of the key concepts that they submit to scrutiny are screening, early identification and the teaching objectives approach. They point out that screening is a term borrowed from medicine and, as in medicine and social services work, its basic purpose is to locate those children who may need special help. It implies, in its most rigorous form that, (a) the whole population of children should be examined, (b) those showing unusual scores or levels of performance be then subjected to further, more detailed examination to determine the exact nature and extent of their difficulties, and (c) some appropriate remediation be supplied. The concept of screening also seems to entail prediction about the effects of unremediated development. And it is this notion of prediction of future performance that has served to throw into question for some people the very notion of screening. As Gipps *et al.* put it, 'identification and prediction of children at risk is a far less precise process than the identification of . . . physical conditions' and for this reason 'screening in this area [education] has not been as successful as it has been in medicine' (ibid., p.16). They argue that because educational screening has been commonly associated with prediction of future educational progress, and because prediction has often been so poor, especially in relation to later reading skills, it has caused educational psychologists to view the procedure with some scepticism. However, this scepticism has had a positive outcome. It has led to a placing of emphasis on the ' accurate description of a child's actual accomplishments at the time of assessment. This move away from dire concern about the future to concern about the present is more than a mere change of emphasis. (It could, after all, be argued that this concern with the present is itself fuelled by the knowledge that current difficulties are pointers to later, and educationally more damaging, handicaps.) It is indeed more than a mere change of emphasis because the name given to it, viz. early identification, is intended to signify to the teacher specific weaknesses that lie behind, or are causative of, current slowness or retardation in currently significant areas of development or, in the case of four to six year olds, in coping with the nursery curriculum.

The assessment instruments that might be used in an 'early identification' approach or model are likely to differ, therefore, from those that would be used for 'prediction' purposes. The latter would imply a thorough understanding of the linkages and the hierarchical relationships among skills and abilities far removed from one another in time and far removed from one another in terms of their superficial characteristics. Screening and prediction at, to take an extreme example, four years of age related to likely competence in reading at nine years of age would not involve many of the skills and competencies required of, and displayed by, a reader aged nine. Four year olds do not have the vocabulary, the range of semantic references, the cognitive abilities, the interests and the particular motivations of nine year olds. Highly accurate prediction at age four of a nine year old's reading accuracy, reading speed and reading comprehension would therefore have to be based on social, perceptual and cognitive skills (a) that on theoretical and/or empirically determined grounds were known to be indispensable pre-requisites, and (b) that were reliably measurable at age four. The fact is that these conditions cannot yet be met, and certainly not for congenitally blind and partially sighted children.

Confidence in the validity of assessment methods is, of course, greater in relation to a pre-schooler's present stage of development and to his existing problems and competencies. Psychologists and pre-school advisory staff are routinely using checklists and developmental scales for picking up those children who are experiencing difficulties, or showing retardation, in areas of functioning that are relevant to what is currently being done or taught at home or in playgroups or nurseries. The emphasis, then, in the early identification model is very much on the kind of immediate remediation, intervention, that is required for present activities. In this approach, the link between the assessment procedure and the subsequent action is both closer in time and in its logical and psychological relationship to the tasks and skills required from the child. And with the pre-school infant, there is often a specificity about some of the behaviour in question that makes it somewhat easier to analyse and shape up. In the case, for example, of the blind infant who fails to search for a toy or other object he has dropped — with all the loss of information about the world that such an event and such a failure can entail — it is relatively simple in principle to devise ways of promoting search behaviour and making it rewarding for the child. Here, assessment and remediation are seen to proceed simultaneously.

Very similar to the early identification approach is the teaching objectives approach. Again, there is the close proximity of assessment and remedial action. As with programmed learning, the emphasis is on fine-grained analysis of the task, specification of objectives in operational or behavioural terms, and the shaping-up of the desired behaviour through a series of small steps, with immediate reinforcement of correct responses and the correction of incorrect ones. There is a concern with establishing the criterion or standard to be aimed at, rather than with placing the child and his accomplishments on some kind of normative scale or continuum. It is essentially, then, a criterion-referenced approach to the assessment procedure, and does not necessarily entail the prior development of universally applicable, objectively valid and highly reliable test instruments. Or at least it seems not to; nevertheless, when the logic of the approach is examined, it does pre-suppose a sound understanding of what is reasonable to expect of a given age and stage of physical, physiological, anatomical and mental development. In other words, there is a sub-stratum that cannot be separated from the notion of normative performance: at its simplest, one does not expect of four year olds what one would expect of nine year olds.

Procedures and instruments specifically developed for identifying and assessing the needs of visually handicapped children at the pre-school stage

One of the hard-won outcomes of their working lives among professionals responsible for assessing young children is the building up of a kind of internal checklist against which they measure a child, his behaviour and his environment. This internal checklist is the product of knowledge about child development (with all its hidden, 'normative' sub-strata) and of the assessor's own experience, the latter being itself an amalgam, based upon such observational practices as noting: how and whether the child uses his near and distance vision; the apparent width of the visual field; the content and quality of language; the child's and the family's acceptance of the visual disability; the presence of manneristic behaviours. It comes, too, from what may be described as a general alertness, awareness or sensitivity on the part of the tester that facilitates the registering of nuances of verbal and non-verbal behaviour, of attitudes and of other personality characteristics that may help to 'explain' some aspects of performance.

In addition to these informal procedures for assessing a child, there are various formal observational methods that are highly objective, in the sense that their use by different observers will produce the same, or very nearly the same, record of what occurred. They are the traditional event-sampling, time-sampling and diary methods of the child psychologist, the advantages of which will be discussed later. These procedures can extend the information obtainable from three instruments that have been specifically designed for use with blind and partially sighted children in the age range 0–5 years (Reynell, 1979) and 0–6 years (Maxfield and Buchholz, 1957) and the Oregon Project (Brown et al., 1986).

The oldest of these inventories or scales is the Maxfield–Buchholz Social Maturity Scale for Blind Pre-school Children, designed to assess the personal and social development of such children. The current version is an adaptation of the original Edgar Doll 'Vineland Social Maturity Scale' (Doll, 1953). It differs from its progenitor in a number of ways, principally in the age range of children for whom it is intended and, of course, in its attempt to take account of the handicapping consequences of blindness. Although it is not arranged in the form of separate sub-scales, there are in fact seven areas of development that are being assessed. They are:

- self-help and self-care, general;
- self-help and self-care, eating;
- self-help and self-care, dressing;
- self-help and self-care, communication;
- self-help and self-care, socialization;
- self-help and self-care, occupation;
- self-help and self-care, locomotor.

Up to the age of 12 months, the items, which are checked by direct observation and discussion with the care-givers, are to do:

- with physical development (e.g. rolling over, moving about on flat surfaces in one fashion or another and sitting unsupported for several minutes);

- with simple interactions with adults (e.g. responding to a familiar person, demanding attention and imitating speech patterns);
- and with manipulation of, and interest in, objects (e.g. grasping small object which comes in contact with hand, releases objects with contact, showing active curiosity about objects in the environment).

A total of 95 items leads up to age six, with later items being concerned with self-help and care skills, receptive and expressive language development, social interactions, and self-directed exploratory and adaptive behaviour. The authors made no claims about the predictive validity of the instrument, stressing that it was 'not an intelligence test ... [but, rather] it is an inventory of the social competence of the young blind child ... based on the performance of other blind children in the same age range' (Maxfield and Buchholz, 1957, p.3). Nevertheless, Gillman and Goddard (1974) found a significant correlation between Maxfield–Buchholz Social Quotient scores, as measured before age six, and IQ as measured after the age of six among a small group of blind children.

It has been dismissed by Bradley-Johnson (1986) as 'pre-Sputnik and unlikely to be applicable today'. This seems to be unjustified, since practitioners still find it helpful in deciding whether early intervention and remedial programmes should be instituted and, of course, while space exploration may have changed dramatically in the post-Sputnik era, children are still the same species, with much the same needs and skills. It can prove valuable for obtaining a global impression of a blind child's general level of development (a Social Age and Social Quotient can be calculated) and it can pinpoint specific lags, e.g. failure to move around a familiar room unattended before the age of two or to initiate own play activity by the age of three.

Much more extensively used nowadays in Great Britain are the 'Developmental Scales for Young Visually Handicapped Children – Part 1, Mental Development', usually referred to as the Reynell–Zinkin Scales (Reynell, 1979). After the initial development work was carried out in the 1970s, further trials were undertaken with a sample of 109 children. The scales are modestly described in the introduction to the manual as designed 'to enable professional people, concerned with young visually handicapped children, to have some guidelines for assessment and developmental advice', this advice to be offered 'to the parents, or to whoever has responsibility for the children's daily care' (ibid., p.11). The age range is from about three months of age up to five years, and as with the Maxfield—Buchholz Scale the information is mainly obtained by interview with the child's carer and by direct observation of behaviour in the home or nursery school.

Although the manual describes, in summary fashion, the motor scales, these have not yet, in fact, been published. They are reported to be oriented 'towards estimating the hand function and locomotion necessary in order that the child's motor ability should not hold up the learning processes'. The published mental scales have six sub-scales, viz:

- Social Adaptation (SA);
- Sensori-Motor Understanding (SM);
- Exploration of Environment (EE);
- Response to Sound and Verbal Comprehension (VC);
- Expressive Language – Structure (EL(S));
- Expressive Language – Vocabulary and Content (EL(C));
  (+ 'Communication Sub-scale', not having age scores and used with multi-handicapped subjects.)

For each sub-scale, it is possible to convert the raw score into an age equivalent score, and it suggested by the authors

that the age score tables may be useful in the following ways:

(1)   As an indication of the rate of progress of an individual child.
(2)   As an indication of specific areas of difficulty at any stage.
(3)   To compare the rate of development of a particular child with that of others in a comparable visual category. (Ibid., p.46)

Separate conversion tables are provided for blind and partially sighted children, but of course the methods of assigning children to vision categories at this early age are by no means very reliable, and the authors have themselves said that 'it would probably be more descriptive of our samples if they were labelled "severe" and "very severe" in visual handicap rather than "partially sighted" and "blind"'. They point out, too, 'that vision, and use of vision, changed in many of the children as they got older, with the changes varying either way'. (It must also be emphasized that these Reynell–Zinkin Scales are not themselves tests of vision.) Possibly in an attempt to ensure that the scales are not used for predictive purposes, the authors state that the

categories 'blind' and 'partially sighted' used here should not be confused with the educational categories established later on. The division was based on the presence or absence of visually directed reaching for objects on the table. If reaching was clearly visually guided, they were put into the 'partially sighted' group. If they groped around, finding the object mainly by touch, they were put into the 'blind' group.

There is also a table for sighted children, thus making it possible for users to compare a given child (a) with children in the same vision group, (b) with children in the other visual disability group, and (c) with fully sighted children. For health visitors, social workers and peripatetic teachers, the tables are useful as they make it possible to give reassurance to parents, especially in families where there are other, fully sighted, children who tend to reach important developmental milestones much earlier. Examples are going up and downstairs by any method; typically, sighted children are doing this at about 15 months of age, whereas blind children are aged 24 to 30 months when these skills and competences usually begin to appear.

The Maxfield – Buchholz and Reynell – Zinkin Scales differ from each other in a number of ways, and this points up their possibly complementary usefulness. First of all, the Maxfield – Buchholz is specifically for blind children in the age range 0 – 6 years, although it seems clear from the Guide to Its Use that only a small proportion of the sample of 484 was totally blind; it is worth noting, too, that a large number of the subjects were premature and their visual impairment was attributed to retrolental fibroplasia. The Reynell – Zinkin has been designed for assessing both blind and partially sighted children aged 0 – 5 years.

Secondly, the Reynell – Zinkin is scored in terms of its six separate sub-scales, whereas the Maxfield – Buchholz provides merely global Social Age and Social Quotient scores. It would appear, therefore, that the Reynell – Zinkin allows for the drawing of a 'profile' and the Maxfield – Buchholz does not. It has already been observed, however, that every item in the Maxfield – Buchholz is labelled as belonging to one of seven categories, viz:

- Self-help, general;
- Self-help, dressing;
- Self-help, eating;
- Communication;
- Socialization;
- Locomotion;
- Occupation.

This would make it possible, in principle at least, to use the Maxfield – Buchholz for drawing up a similar kind of behavioural and developmental profile.

Thirdly, the content of the two scales varies in some interesting ways, as is partly suggested by the categories. The Reynell – Zinkin has three of its six main sub-scales devoted to some aspect of language development, and of the 130 or so items in the test, nearly 60 per cent are designed to elicit information about language. In the Maxfield – Buchholz, on the other hand, of the 85 items allocated to the same age range, viz. birth to age five, only 12 or 14 per cent are concerned with communication, which is the nearest category to the three Reynell – Zinkin language sub-scales. Forty-five per cent of the Maxfield – Buchholz items in the same age range are concerned with self-help, and one-fifth, or 20 per cent, of all Maxfield – Buchholz items up to age five years are specifically related to dressing and eating as compared with less than half that percentage in the Reynell – Zinkin Scales.

Fourthly, the scales differ in the degree of detailed information they provide on how to administer the items and evaluate the quality of the responses or other behaviours. The Reynell – Zinkin is perhaps somewhat less detailed, and this may be because it is pre-supposed that it will be administered and interpreted by those who 'should have a sound understanding of early intellectual development, and some understanding of how this deviates in visually handicapped children' (ibid., p.12). This is again reinforced when the authors go on to say that the 'scoring is not rigid, but depends very much on the examiner's understanding of the early stages of intellectual development'. The Maxfield – Buchholz Guide, however, also states that it can be used most effectively by those already having considerable experience in the psychological testing of small children and in the diagnostic interviewing of children and their parents. Nevertheless, the overall impression is that the Maxfield – Buchholz Guide is somewhat more informative and more precise than the Reynell – Zinkin in terms of the degree of detailed instructions it provides concerning administration and interpretation of the test items.

The scales thus differ in some substantive ways. The Reynell – Zinkin's preponderance of language-related behaviours (60 per cent) is no doubt related to the first author's interest and extensive research in this area of human development with non-handicapped children, and it enables her to show differences between the visually handicapped and the sighted, and between the blind and partially sighted. Some interesting inferences are drawn about the causation and patterning of the divergences. For the psychologist and the peripatetic teacher, Reynell's arguments are of considerable significance since they point not only to what she conceives as the handicapping sequelae of visual impairment but also to the kinds of remediation and intervention that might be called for. She is, too, sufficiently clear-cut as to the timing and the likely emergence of the differences as to make it possible to prepare for them. As an example, she shows how the blind are behind the partially sighted in verbal comprehension at the stage of relating two objects to each other in response to such commands as 'Put the spoon in the cup.'

In these and other areas where her work has convinced her that there are regularly observable differences, she stresses the need for early and intensive help, suggesting that such help take the form of making the associations between objects and their verbal labels, and of relating language to concrete situations. She says that while teaching cannot completely make up for the co-ordinating function of vision, it must 'be directed towards this ... co-ordinating function, such as linking object to object, and word to object, using whatever sensory modalities are available to the child'. As an example, she urges that 'instead of just talking about a "brush" the child needs to handle it, use it, and hear the label "brush" at the same time' and she says that this 'should be repeated at every appropriate time during daily living activities', with the parents being used as teachers under professional guidance, with a professional visit being made once in every six weeks.

It is perhaps in this pinpointing of differences and in the suggestions about subsequent action that the Reynell–Zinkin Scales are superior to the Maxfield–Buchholz Scales, although it would be unfair to ignore similar if implicit advice that is contained in the notes on scoring standards in the Maxfield–Buchholz Guide.

Between them, these two assessment instruments constitute a basic tool-kit for teachers, psychologists and other professional advisers working with families in which there is a pre-school, visually handicapped child. That is not to say that they are completely comprehensive in their coverage. They are less than adequate for the seriously multi-handicapped, visually impaired child, and there are areas of functioning for the 'ordinary' visually handicapped child which they do not assess at all. They are not, either, as useful as the Oregon Project for drawing up a programme of remediation.

The Oregon Project for Visually Impaired and Blind Pre-school Children (Brown *et al.*, 1986) is nevertheless similar in many respects to the other two instruments. The main difference is that it was quite specifically designed as a combined assessment and teaching package for use by those working with children in the age range 0–6 years. The OR's emphasis on linking assessment to immediate teaching springs from its origins in the Portage Project, a home-based system in which specialist help is offered to the parents of handicapped children by means of regular home visits; during these visits the trained specialist discusses and practises with the parent the next set of skills and behaviours judged to be feasible for the child (*vide*, for example, Daly *et al.*, 1985). The devisers of the OR Project espoused this key feature of the Portage philosophy, claiming that the 'materials are particularly suited to a home-based mode of delivery of services' (Brown *et al.*, 1986, p.xi).

The assessment inventory comprises 695 items, spread over six areas of development, viz:

- cognitive;
- language;
- self-help;
- socialization;
- fine-motor skills;
- gross-motor skills.

In terms of its validity and reliability, there must be some caution since only 75 visually impaired children took part in the field testing (as compared with a final sample of 109 children for the Reynell–Zinkin Scales and 484 for the Maxfield–Buchholz Social Maturity Scale). Somewhat greater confidence can perhaps be placed in the technical suitability of the six content areas and the individual test items as they draw extensively upon the corpus of knowledge built up over the years by psychologists, paediatricians and other researchers in the field of early childhood development.

The OR inventory would seem to be both more comprehensive in its coverage and more finely detailed than the other two scales, having six times as many items. There is, however, considerable overlap among the OR sub-scales. For example, 'Laughs and smiles' is an item in the Language sub-scale for the age level 0–1 years, while 'Smiles in response to attention by familiar person', a slightly more specific variant of the same piece of behaviour, is located in the Socialization sub-scale for the 0–1 year age level. Similarly, item 1 in the Socialization area, 'Quiets or changes body movement in response to touch, sight, or sound of familiar person', will also lead to the recording in the inventory of the achievement of item 2 in the Language sub-scale, viz. 'Quiets or changes body movement in response to sound (stops movement of or moves head, arm, or leg)'. It should be noted that there is not complete reciprocity; the requirement for 'by a familiar person' suggests a more advanced discrimination by the infant. Nevertheless, the observed occurrence of the behaviours involving the 'familiar person' may automatically lead to the recording of achievement of a skill in another area of development. This is an advantage possessed by the OR inventory. It does not necessarily mean that it is a much more informative instrument than the others. Its format, for example, does not easily lead to the useful distinction between expressive and receptive language skills which is possible with the Reynell – Zinkin procedures, nor among the various self-help skills identified in the Maxfield – Buchholz Scale as Self-help, general; Self-help, dressing; and Self-help, eating.

Table 3.1 brings out something of the particular biases and emphases of these three instruments as they are currently constructed (it needing to be borne in mind that the R – Z Scales are still lacking the Part 2 – Motor Development sub-scales). Although the M – B Scale is characterized by its concern with Self-help skills, with 46, or half of its 95, items dealing with eating, dressing, and general self-help and self-care skills, there are 128 items of this kind in the OR inventory, but they constitute less than one-fifth of the total number. In this area of development, the R – Z and M – B Scales are not so 'fine-grained' as the OR, but examination of the OR items must inevitably give rise to questions about the usefulness of some of them: 'Opens mouth for breast, bottle, or spoon', and 'Sucks and swallows liquid' are behaviours which are included in the skills inventory but which do not have counterparts in R – Z and M – B, presumably on the grounds that they are so basic as not to warrant recording. Another major difference is in the age-placement of some skills, with R – Z and M – B generally pointing to skills occurring later than is expected by the authors of the OR inventory, an example being the infant's attempts to feed himself with a spoon which M – B and R – Z suggest is typical of a visually impaired child at the end of the second year of life while the OR inventory has this in the first year.

The nature and size of the samples used in the field trials may account for such differences. The practical significance of these disparities is that a child's failure to achieve competence in the skills at the times suggested in an inventory may result in disappointment and anxiety in his parents. (Our present inability to be more informative about ages and stages of some of the visually impaired child's developing competences is a reflection of the unsatisfactory technical reliability of the existing measurement scales. The developers of these instruments are beset by the difficulties arising from the low incidence of severe congenital visual impairment, from the high incidence of additional disabilities, and from the great variation in the levels of residual vision among the target population. Given these less than perfect correlations among the scales, advisers need to be familiar with the content of all of them so that they can be properly conservative in making judgements about a child's development.)

Undoubtedly the great strength of the OR Project is its linking of assessment with suggestions for teaching activities. The project provides a comprehensive listing of things to be done and said by care-givers, the child and his siblings that seem well-founded in conventional practice and that make distinctions between the needs of totally blind infants and those with some sight.

Procedures not specifically designed for visually impaired children

As noted, the technical difficulties associated with standardizing any assessment procedures are compounded in the field of visual handicap by the low incidence of visual impairment and by the unfortunate fact that so many of the target population have additional physical and mental disabilities. Defining the group as those without any other significant handicaps would only serve to reduce the size of the population even further, and make the ensuing tests unsuitable for perhaps half of the pupils in nurseries and schools specializing in the education of children suffering from severe visual impairment; if the tests are also to be used only with those who are either totally blind or have perception of light, then the problems of devising, trialling and validating the procedures are again increased. Fortunately, the handicapping consequences of the impairment cannot hide the fact that these children are children, similar in most respects to their fully sighted peers. For this reason, it is possible and even desirable for them to be assessed in many areas of development with the same test instruments as are used with their sighted age peers.

One such instrument is the *Keele Pre-school Assessment Guide* (Tyler, 1980). It is for individual administration and its purpose is described as the identification of the educational needs of 'normal' children in the age range three to five years. The developmental areas covered are language, cognition, socialization and physical skills. Inevitably, some activities and skills are not applicable to blind children, and the scores that can be derived by use of the Guide will be of less value to nursery school teachers than the qualitative information about the child's usual behaviours. It has been designed to point to appropriate teaching/learning objectives of the kind that have meaning for parents

Table 3.1 Special assessment procedures for pre-school children

Scales/ tests	Skills and behaviours covered (numbers of items in sub-scale)						
1. Reynell– Zinkin scales: Developmental scales for young visually handicapped children. Part 1, Mental Development (0–5 yrs) (Windsor: NFER-NELSON)	Social Adaptation (18)	Sensori-Motor Understanding (23)	Exploration of Environment (12)	Response to Sound and Verbal Comprehension (36)	Vocalization and Expressive Language Structure (22)	Expressive Language Vocabulary and Content (18)	Communication: No age scores; provided only as addition to main sub-scales 'as a guide for teaching children who may have combined visual and auditory handicaps' 20 items for proving receptive and expressive communication in such children
2. Social Maturity Scale for Blind Pre-school Children by K.E. Maxfield and S. Buchholz (0–6 yrs) (NY: AFB)	Self-help, General (24)	Self-help Eating (9)	Self-help, Dressing (15)	Communication (12)	Locomotor (11)	Socialization (16)	Occupation (14)
	N.B. Items arranged in year groups and not as separate sub-scales						
3. Oregon Project for Visually Impaired and Blind Pre-school Children (0–6 yrs) (Medford: Jackson Education Service District)	Cognitive (157)	Language (130)	Self-help (128)	Socialization (87)	Fine Motor (94)	Gross Motor (99)	

and other care-givers. A similar instrument, also published by NFER-NELSON is *Assessment in Nursery Education* by Bate and Smith (1986). This covers the same age range and evaluates performance in 'social skills, talking and listening, manual and tool skills, thinking and doing and physical skills'. Again, many items would be inappropriate for blind and partially sighted children (e.g. walking along a balance bar) but there are others (e.g. threading beads) where observing the child as he tackles the task can provide useful information about residual vision, attention span, perseverance, and fine-motor and tactual skills.

The Schedule of Growing Skills (Bellman and Cash, 1987) is described as a developmental screening procedure. The 180 items of the schedule are grouped into nine skill areas, based upon the earlier work of the famous paediatrician, Mary Sheridan. The numerical scores in the nine areas are converted into a graphical Profile, copies of which can be sent to other professional workers. The comprehensive coverage of the schedule makes it a potentially useful instrument for pre-school advisers because its foundation in the notion of normal development can bring out some of the anomalies that may be associated with visual impairment.

There are other non-specialist instruments that can be used with visually handicapped pre-schoolers. Some of these, spanning a much wider age range, are examined in the next chapter which is concerned with assessment of children at school.

CHAPTER 4

Blind and Partially Sighted Pupils of School Age

Having argued in the previous chapter that there are good grounds for using non-specialized tests with visually handicapped pre-schoolers, it may seem contradictory for the writer now to point up the dangers of using such procedures with the child of school age. There is, however, one important difference between the two age groups when assessment is being considered. Few pre-school tests are timed. That is, no time limits are usually required for the completion of individual items within the test or for completion of the test in its entirety. Attention is directed towards assessing the child's 'power' or ability. At school age, and especially in tests of intelligence, time limits are usually set, and what is being measured is a mixture of power and speed. As will be demonstrated later, one of the most commonly observed consequences of blindness or severe visual impairment is a slower pick-up of information, either on account of the essentially linear, sequential nature of tactual perception (blind subjects) or on account of the restricted width of the perceptual 'window' or the blurred images (partially sighted subjects). In a timed test that has been designed and standardized for use with normally sighted learners, the visually handicapped child is therefore likely to be at a considerable disadvantage, even if items have been converted into braille or large-print format. Even when there are no time limits, or when additional time allowances are granted, the fact that the tasks are going to take longer will introduce new elements into the situation, viz. fatigue and its effects upon quality of performance on the later, more difficult items in the test battery. In espousing the general case for visually handicapped pupils to be taught and assessed in the same manner as their non-disabled peers, we must try not to further exacerbate the educationally handicapping effects of their disability. In this chapter, a description and evaluation of specialized tests, that take account of the disability, will be made first, and then some non-specialist instruments, that have been used from time to time, will be presented.

Specialized tests

Williams Intelligence Test for children with defective vision

The Williams Test (Williams, 1956) is the only British intelligence test that has been standardized for use with visually handicapped children over the whole school age range. The population for whom it is intended consists of children aged 3.5 to 16.0 years, with visual acuities ranging upwards from nil to 6/60 Snellen (and up to 6/36 Snellen where there is a narrowing of the field of vision). The measure contains a separate, 40-item vocabulary test almost identical with the vocabulary sub-scale of the original 1949 version of the Wechsler Intelligence Scale for Children (the WISC). As in administering any test to a child with defective sight, users of the Williams find it is important to make the instructions clear and unambiguous, to use voice intonation and stress changes for signalling beginnings and endings of tasks, to remove the sources of extraneous sounds, and in the few items that are timed or presented only once, to make these requirements clearly understood in advance. Few items require knowledge of braille but for those that do, the examiner must be prepared to spend some time to become knowledgeable about the kinds of reversal or inversion errors that a child might make. Despite the fact that the test has now been in use for so long, little information is available about validity and reliability. On the basis of the writer's own extended investigations of cognitive development and school achievement in visually impaired children, significant individual changes in IQ have sometimes been observed when the test has been re-administered, but set against these individual variations, there has nevertheless been a satisfactory overall test/retest correlation over a two-year period of $+0.89$ (N = 99).

The test is for individual administration; that is, only one child at a time can be assessed, duration of the testing being generally of the order of 45 to 70 minutes. This time is heavily dependent upon the tester's skill or good fortune in choosing the right 'basal' item at which to start. In a 100-item test such as the Williams, spanning a wide age range, the practice is to start testing at a 'point where the child, while making some enjoyable effort, is likely to succeed' (Williams, 1956). The manual provides guidelines for determining the appropriate starting point, the major criteria being chronological age and performance on a separate vocabulary test. Termination of testing occurs when eight consecutive items have been failed. (In practice, duration of the test is often extended beyond what seems to be the child's natural 'ceiling' as a result of scattered successes among a string of failures.)

The items are arranged in ascending order of difficulty and are predominantly verbal although there are four unscored 'performance' items located within the first 20. These four are described as providing variety for the younger children, and consist of sorting buttons on the basis of size, matching small three-dimensional objects and wooden geometrical formboards, and identifying the missing parts of familiar, everyday objects. Within the main body of the test there are two bead chain tasks that have a significant 'performance' element in them, the child being required to remember and then re-construct a chain of beads of various shapes made up initially by the tester. The bulk of the task is, nevertheless, rightly classified as verbal, in the sense that the principal stimulus mode and the principal response mode involve words. The main processes tapped are:

- reasoning (primarily similarities and social reasoning);
- short-term memory (immediate recall of digits and sentences, tactual recognition);
- spatial imagery ('visualization' of clock face, directionality);
- retrieval and application of knowledge (early number skills, verbal fluency and comprehension, and word definition).

While the items are not labelled or grouped under these headings, it may be helpful to conceptualize them in such a manner, particularly for those test users who view intelligence in terms of separate categories or sub-scales. This allows a 'profile' to be drawn for each child, showing relative strengths and weaknesses and providing a more qualitative assessment than is possible from the mere calculation of an IQ score or score range.

The raw score is transformed into an intelligence quotient without reference to 'mental age', the tables in the manual enabling this to be done easily through consideration of the raw score and the child's chronological age. The quotient is based upon a mean score of 100 and a standard deviation of 15. In effect, this means that a child can be compared with a representative group of visually handicapped children of his own age. Some 68 per cent of this group will have intelligence quotients between 85 and 115, with about 16 per cent being below an IQ of 85 and another 16 per cent being above an IQ of 115. What cannot legitimately be done is to assert that a child assigned, for example, an intelligence quotient of 118 is in some general way clearly more intelligent than a child of the same age whose raw score corresponds to a quotient of 113; nor, indeed, that a fall of five IQ points between two testings of the same child represents a deterioration in intelligence. Scores on this kind of test, despite the care taken in the devising of items and in the selection of representative samples of children at different ages, are not absolutely self-consistent, variations from one occasion to another being due to all sorts of factors (some of them to do with the test giver, some to do with the test taker, and some to do with the conditions under which the test is administered). There is, therefore, what is technically known as an 'error component' in the score obtained on any given occasion. An estimate can be made of the likely magnitude of this error component. In the Williams Test, data obtained by the writer (Tobin, 1978) in a longitudinal investigation of cognitive development and school achievement suggest that one may be 70 per cent confident that the child's 'true score' lies in a range running from five points below to five points above the score actually obtained (and 95 per cent confident that it is in a range running from 10 points below to 10 points above that obtained score). Differences between children, and between two scores for any one child, must therefore be interpreted in the light of this 'confidence interval', and should certainly not be evaluated as very significant or meaningful if they fall inside this margin of error. Indeed, as mentioned earlier, users of tests like the Williams are well advised to think of test scores as ranges rather than exact points, and good practice would consist of quoting this range or 'confidence interval' when discussing and communicating the results of a single administration of the test. The point being made is that while the score actually obtained is the best estimate of the true or real score, by giving a band or range, test designers are publicly recognizing the elasticity of the measuring procedures and alerting other users of the information (parents, administrators and other professionals) not to make facile comparisons between children or between an individual child's performance on the same test at different times.

Blind Learning Aptitude Test (BLAT)

The BLAT is a 49-item, embossed and raised-line test that has been in gestation for many years, and that has attracted a good deal of attention in the United States throughout the whole of the period, largely because psychologists and teachers were hopeful that it would throw light on aspects of blind children's aptitudes and potential that were not being illuminated by existing tests of intelligence and achievement. Its author,

43

Figure 4.1 An example of the kind of item used in the Blind Learning Aptitude Test (NB this is not a copy of an actual item in the BLAT)

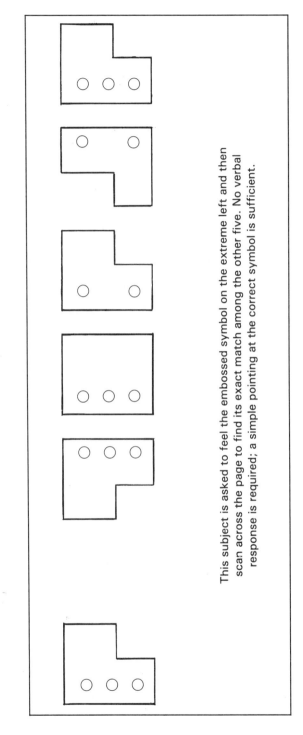

This subject is asked to feel the embossed symbol on the extreme left and then scan across the page to find its exact match among the other five. No verbal response is required; a simple pointing at the correct symbol is sufficient.

Professor T. Ernest Newland of the University of Illinois, had strongly and publicly espoused the notion, and the importance, of evaluating 'process' rather than 'product', and had set himself the task of constructing a measuring instrument that would measure the psychological operations fundamental to learning. He was unhappy with existing intelligence tests for the blind (most of which were adaptations of well-known 'sighted' test) such as Hayes–Bint tests and the WISC, which he considered to be primarily concerned with 'product', i.e. with achievement and specific information.

The test (Newland, 1971) makes use of abstract symbols, rather larger than the conventional braille cell, and the child is required to recognize and discriminate, and to make associations and deductions from and among these symbols without any recourse to memory and with relatively little reliance on verbal competence.

There are, in effect, six groups of items, each of which is introduced by two non-scoring trial items. In the first group, the child is required to find the odd one among six tactile shapes; for example, the circle among an array of different sized triangles, squares and other rectilinear shapes. The second group requires the finding of a shape similar to the one on the extreme left of the array, what is called a 'matching-to-sample' task. The next demands the recognition of the existence of a series or progression; three items constitute the basis of the progression (in which, for instance, there may be a systematic angular rotation of the shapes) and the task consists of finding the next shape in the series from a set of six possible shapes. The fourth group comprises patterns/matrices that have to be completed by selection of one shape from an adjoining array; there is a precisely defined relationship among the shapes in the matrix, and only one of the adjoining set satisfies this logically definable relationship. The five items of the fifth group have one large, incomplete outline or textured pattern in each case, and there are six options that have to be felt in order to locate the missing piece of the large shape. The last group or sub-section has elements in common with earlier ones. There is a three-row by three-column matrix of small shapes, and there is again a logically definable relationship among the units within each row and within each column; the ninth unit is missing and can be found in an adjacent set of six shapes, the child being able to use either the row or the column relationship for identifying the missing unit. Within each sub-section there is what the deviser describes as a 'rough order of increasing difficulty', and testing is normally terminated after five successive errors within a series, whereupon the next group is tackled.

The test has been standardized on what would seem, from the test manual, to be a sufficiently large and representative sample of North

American children who suffer from severe visual impairment. However, the technical adequacy has been questioned in part by Bradley-Johnson (1986) who does not believe it is a geographically representative sample and who is not satisfied with the split between pupils from integrated and special schools. The instructions for administration are comprehensive and unambiguous, and the tables supplied in the manual are intended to enable users to obtain 'learning quotients' and 'learning aptitude age equivalents'.

There are some other drawbacks to the instrument. Some of these the deviser has himself acknowledged in the manual. He sees it as 'constituting only the first stage in the development of a measure of the learning aptitude of blind children'; states that 'much work is needed to refine it'; and draws attention to certain specific questions that users of the BLAT will wish to pose. This recognition of possible criticisms is a virtue in itself and a guide to those who might wish to use and interpret it. The present writer's own reservations are in line with many of the points made by the designer/author, but there are also aspects that give rise to quite substantial disagreements over the inferences to be drawn from the published statistical data.

The first of these is to do with validity. The deviser has approached this in a number of ways but essentially they are mainly to do with concurrent validity. One is in terms of improvement in performance in step with increase in age; the second is in terms of positive but not perfect correlations with certain IQ tests; and the third is in terms of positive correlations with measured educational achievement. Satisfactory results have been produced in the first area, but these do not show, of themselves, that BLAT is measuring learning aptitude, but merely that older children do better than younger ones; such improvement can prove nothing about learning aptitude as such (at least in the absence of other evidence). The high correlations for the second area (relationships between BLAT and Hayes – Binet and WISC Verbal) could mean either that BLAT is an intelligence test like them or that they are learning aptitude tests like BLAT! In the third area, the BLAT is shown to have lower correlations than the IQ tests with various aspects of school achievement (i.e. actual measures of learning). No other external criteria are used and in one sense therefore the only 'proof' that the BLAT is measuring learning aptitude is the fact that it has been constructed in accordance with the designer's conceptualization of what learning aptitude is. This is something less than convincing, even to those who might sympathize with this notion. Clearly more objective evidence is needed to support the claim that BLAT is indeed measuring what it purports to measure.

A second cause of rather less concern is in relation to reliability.

Newland reports an overall test-retest correlation co-efficient of +0.865 over a seven-month period. This is somewhat lower than the standard normally aimed at by the National Foundation for Educational Research in the UK, and suggests, among other things, that some 25 per cent of the variance in the second testing is not being accounted for from the first test. Internal consistency is considerably more satisfactory (a Kuder-Richardson type formula giving 0.934).

Despite the reservations that have been outlined above, this test could be most useful to educators and psychologists working with blind children in all English-speaking countries. It has the advantage of a relatively low verbal content, and therefore very few changes would have to be made in the instructions to be given to the children. It is, too, the only standardized instrument of its kind that consists entirely of tactile symbols. It is claimed to be 'culture fair' and thus does not discriminate for or against specific groups of children, and this in itself is of some significance for the many blind pupils coming into schools from immigrant families. The fact that it is sufficiently different (in terms of common or shared variance) from existing tests of intelligence, aptitude or achievement is also a point in its favour, since this suggests that it is measuring something different from them; it may therefore be found to be a useful complement to them, thus putting users in a better position to obtain a more rounded or complete assessment of a child's potential.

There has been more recent support for these claims, Mason and Shukla (1992) having described extensive trials of this assessment procedure in the UK and in India, in which they have compared their results with the data from the original standardization in the USA. In the UK, 100 children in the age range 5.5 to 16.5 years were tested, and in India 320 children in residential, Hindi-speaking schools were used, the age range being 7.5 to 15.5 years. These researchers fully support Newland's claim that the BLAT is culturally fair; that is, no differences in achievement were found among the subjects that could be attributed to ethnic or cultural factors. They go on to conclude that

> the BLAT can be used with confidence to assess visually impaired children for various purposes such as screening for admission to other schools/colleges, grouping for special educational programmes, predicting academic performance and educational/ vocational guidance. (Mason and Shukla, 1992, p.98)

Reading tests

The psychologist, teacher and peripatetic adviser who needs to assess tactual reading skills has three tests available. All three can be administered straight from the manuals even by those who know no braille. In that case, however, little more can be derived from them than reading ages or quotients. For diagnostic purposes, the tester must be able to read braille sufficiently well to identify the reversal and inversion errors that the braille code can give rise to, since its punctiform, rectilinear format is productive of such errors to a far greater extent than its ink-print counterpart. Furthermore, Standard English Braille consists of a large number of contracted forms, for words as well as for two, three, four and five letter combinations. The rules governing their use − all aimed at reducing bulk and scanning/cover times − are also numerous and complex. Even by early adolescence some children will not have learned all the forms that might occur, especially those with a relatively low frequency of occurrence. The educational psychologist may therefore be tempted to omit the administration of tests of reading or to pass the job over to his teacher colleagues. Where assessment is carried out on a team basis, this may be defended, and even considered beneficial for team morale. In other circumstances, the onus is surely upon the psychologist to acquire the necessary skills. The Royal National Institute for the Blind publishes a Braille Primer in ink-print and this describes the code and lists all the rules. It is not necessary for the tester to be able to read braille by touch; sight reading is all that is required to enable the user to monitor and understand the child's progress on any of the three objective measures that are currently available.

The first, the Tooze Braille Speed Test (Tooze, 1962) is sub-titled 'A test of basic ability in reading braille' and is described in the foreword as a test of basic perceptual ability. It is, however, rather more than this as it requires rapid and accurate identification and labelling of three-letter words printed in Grade 1 Braille; that is, with no contracted forms. The 120 words that make up the test have been selected to avoid the use of contractions and 'to avoid those which might present vocabulary difficulty'. It is a speed test in which the child is asked to read the list of words as quickly as he can and in which he is encouraged to leave any word whose recognition causes him to hesitate for more than five seconds. For comparative purposes, the raw score − the number of words correctly identified in one minute − can be transformed into a reading age, and into a standardized score with a mean of 100 and a standard deviation of 15. Administration and scoring are simple, making it possible for the user to obtain information about a child's familiarity with the elements of uncontracted braille and of his mastery of simple blending and recognition skills. As the author himself puts it, the instrument allows the user 'to make a speedy assessment of a child's tactile attainment in actually reading braille symbols' (ibid., p.6).

Figure 4.2 Extract (in print form) from the Tooze Braille Speed Test (all words are in Grade 1, uncontracted braille). Printed with the permission of the publishers, Association for the Education and Welfare of the Visually Handicapped

CAT	DAD	MAD	EGG	LIP	SUN	LEG	BOY
LOT	CUT	MAP	LIT	JOB	GET	ROB	NAP
WAY	MUG	TAP	MAT	FAT	BUS	COT	BOX
LOG	CAP	FIT	HID	ASK	SIX	TRY	RAG
HOP	RIB	BIT	POP	DIG	CUP	CRY	MAN
GAP	FOX	TOP	GAY	TIP	PUP	PEG	LET
PUT	GOT	TOY	HAM	FAN	BUN	MUD	SOB
BIG	FUR	HIT	BAG	HAT	HOT	DIP	POT
HIP	GUM	RIM	HAS	DID	SUM	FIX	BAT
HAY	MIX	WET	GAS	LAD	WAG	ZIP	NET
SEE	FLY	LAP	FRY	LAY	RAN	RAT	CUB
MAY	SPY	RUG	HUG	RUB	YES	VAN	HUT

Figure 4.3 Extract (in print form) from the Lorimer Recognition Test (all words are in fully contracted Grade 2 braille). Printed with the permission of the publishers, Association for the Education and Welfare of the Visually Handicapped

IT CAN THE BUT LITTLE AND DO WILL LIKE SO
GO NOT HAD OF TO-THE YOU SAID FOR YOUR
THAT MOTHER WITH FROM MUST AS HAVE
THIS HIM PEOPLE IN US INTO THE MORE GOOD
SWING WOULD EVERY DAY CLOTH COULD ITS
UNDER RIGHT OUT ONE ABOUT FATHER WHAT
BY THE SHOULD ARMS SOME AFTER GREAT
CANNOT MEND AGAIN LOUD JUST QUITE SHALL
RATHER BEFORE STUFF BLOW THERE MUCH
CLIFFS VERY PART STILL RIBBON NAME ACROSS
FEED BECAUSE AGAINST ALWAYS BE MANY
HERE SHEET SUCH MYSELF TIME WORK WHICH
BEHIND TODAY BRAILLE WAS HIMSELF WHERE
THROUGH CHILDREN HERSELF LUGGAGE YOUNG
UPON THEIR PADDLE CHOP KNOW TOGETHER
YOURSELF ABOVE KNOWLEDGE POUND EVER

The lower age point of the test is 7 years 3 months, the upper being 12 years 6 months. Pilot testing was undertaken with 135 children and the standardization of the final version with 428 children, such samples representing very large proportions of the total population of blind children in the 7 to 13 year age range. A test-retest correlation co-efficient was calculated, using 68 children from two schools, the resulting co-efficient of +0.975 testifying to the consistency or reliability of the instrument over a three-week period. This tool for assessing one elementary aspect of braille reading has, therefore, much to recommend it: it is simple and quick to administer, easy to score and produces scores (such as reading ages) that teachers are familiar with.

The Lorimer Braille Recognition Test (Lorimer, 1962) supplements this, as its sub-title suggests: 'A test of ability in reading braille contractions'. In his introduction to the test, Lorimer refers to the braille system's 'multitude of symbols and rules' that present 'far more difficulties to a blind child than does the print alphabet to a sighted child'. In this test, he tries to take account of this 'braille factor' in reading by means of a list of some 174 unrelated words and, somewhat over-modestly, seeks to emphasize 'that it does not measure skill in reading; it is concerned only with the ability to feel the shapes, and give the meanings of word-signs and contractions' (ibid., p.5). Of the 189 'signs' of Standard English Braille, 174 appear in the test, the rest being omitted on the grounds of their relative infrequency 'in books normally used by children in the age-range covered by the test' (p.6).

Something of the care and subtlety of the construction can be gleaned from some of the considerations that were borne in mind in the devising of the test. For example, part-word contractions can only be tested through their inclusion in whole words, and it is possible for a child to recognize a very familiar, frequently occurring word even when unsure of the meaning of a contraction contained in the word. A deliberate attempt was made to overcome this problem by the use of words 'not likely to be recognized instantly except by competent readers', correct identification of a given word suggesting, therefore, that the contraction had been registered, decoded and then synthesized with the other symbols/sounds. Unlike the Tooze Speed Test, no overall time limits are set, but if the child cannot identify a word within 10 seconds he is encouraged to move on to the next item, with the test being terminated after eight successive failures. Administration and scoring can be easily completed within 20 minutes, and the raw score can be converted into a reading age and a reading quotient, the latter being based on a mean of 100 and a standard deviation of 15.

The various scores obtainable from the Lorimer Test may be regarded by some users as of less value than some of the other information it can provide. The errors made and even the momentary hesitations over words subsequently correctly identified can indicate to the experienced teacher some of a child's uncertainties related to inversions and reversals of braille shapes, mis-alignment (reading a lower sign as an upper sign), degree of familiarity with the code and its complex rules, as well as level of skill in blending and syllable recognition. As is the case with the Tooze Test, it can be used to observe hand/finger dominance or preference, left-to-right scanning, regressive movements of the reading finger(s), and ability to locate tactually the beginnings and endings of lines, all of which can influence speed of reading.

The manual provides detailed guidance about the conditions under which the test should and should not be administered, and recommends that it be used with children between seven and thirteen years of age. Pilot testing was conducted with a group of 270 children and the final standardization was effected with a sample of 332, representing 'all blind children at school in England and Wales who were between the ages of 7 and 13, had started learning contracted braille, and normally read by touch'. (Lorimer makes a distinction between those blind children who read only by touch and those who have sufficient near vision to see braille and tend to read it by sight when allowed to; the standardization excluded this latter group.) No data are provided on test-retest reliability but the internal consistency of the measure was estimated, using a sub-sample of 110 subjects, and giving rise to a highly satisfactory consistency co-efficient of $+0.99$.

While both these tests can be used by the experienced teacher, who has a detailed knowledge of braille, for more educationally useful purposes than the recording of reading quotients or reading ages, the instructional manuals make it clear that they were not devised to give a comprehensive picture of the child's reading abilities. The Tooze Speed Test contains no contracted braille and is categorically claimed not 'to be a Braille Reading Comprehension Test'. The Lorimer Test of braille contractions is meant 'to provide an instrument for measuring the braille factor' and is specific in declaring that 'it does not measure skill in reading'. Among the dimensions of reading that neither test claims to measure are comprehension and speed of reading of continuous passages of prose. For many years there was no instrument available that could generate such information.

In 1977, the National Foundation for Educational Research attempted to fill this gap by publishing Lorimer's braille adaptation of the well-known 'Neale Analysis of Reading Ability' test (Neale, 1958; 1966; Lorimer, 1977). Neale's original test – for normally sighted children in the age range six to thirteen years – was designed 'to meet a practical need for diagnostic measure'. It consists of six prose passages, varying in length from 26 words at the lowest level to 139 at the highest. In addition, there are three supplementary diagnostic tests involving the names and sounds of letters, auditory discrimination through simple spelling, and blending and recognition of syllables. The prose passages themselves constitute self-contained narratives, graded in content and interest according to the age groups for which each is primarily intended, and the vocabulary is also graded for age on the basis of published wordlists and the empirical testing of the materials. Syntax and length of sentences follow a similar pattern of increasing complexity.

Three measures of reading can be assessed with the Neale, viz. comprehension, accuracy and speed, the raw scores in each case being convertible into reading ages, the range being six years to thirteen, with monthly increments. The test manual provides a considerable amount of information on the validation and normative procedures. Of more immediate interest to the teacher, however, is Neale's emphasis on the diagnostic value of the instrument. For example, in the accuracy sub-scale, six types of errors can be recorded on the answer sheet: mispronunciations, substitutions, refusals, additions, omissions and reversals. These errors, particularly when further broken down by the experienced teacher and tester, can then be used for remedial teaching purposes. The accuracy sub-scale is, in fact, the hub of the test in the sense that the measured levels on the other two sub-scales are largely determined by the child's performance on the former. Testing is terminated when 16 'reading accuracy' errors have been made on a given passage, with reading speed and reading comprehension then being measured up to that point, rather than independently.

Lorimer's standardization of the test with a group of 299 braille readers (Lorimer, 1977) has made it possible for schools to use the same instrument for all their visually handicapped pupils. Apart from the normative data now available for comparing one braille reader with another, Lorimer's work allows users to investigate the nature of a child's reading difficulties, both in terms of the categories of errors identified by Neale and in terms of specific 'braillisms', e.g. misalignments (upper and lower cell signs), sign reversals, missing dots and knowledge of contracted forms. His modifications of the original form of the test consist of: replacement of the picture preceding each passage by an introductory sentence 'read aloud by the examiner just before the child begins to read each narrative ... [and] designed to arouse interest without aiding the child in mechanical reading'; the use of a practice test 'to familiarize the child with the test procedure'; and the extension of Neale's four seconds pause before prompting the next word to a full 12 seconds (on the grounds that braille readers read at about one-third of the pace of ink-print readers). Lorimer's detailed instructions on the administration of the test need, however, to be read in conjunction with the original instructions provided in the manual for the print version of the test.

While Lorimer's painstaking work on the braille version of the Neale Test is a model for others interested in adapting existing instruments, it also highlights the fact that the partially sighted are rarely considered to be in need of similar treatment. Their ability to cope with the print characteristics of tests standardized on a normally sighted population does not prove that they can be regarded as part of that population. Indeed the evidence emerging in a longitudinal study being conducted by the present writer points to substantial deficits in, for example, rate of reading among young readers classified as partially sighted. In normative terms, therefore, the standard Neale Test must be used with the greatest caution; as a diagnostic instrument, however, it is of immediate relevance to the classroom teacher since it can pinpoint specific areas of weakness and can thus be used for drawing up a remedial teaching programme. In due course, if continued use is to be made of it, it must be standardized on the population of print readers suffering from severe visual impairment so that appropriate and accurate comparisons can be made among them.

The Neale Test is nevertheless recommended for the partially sighted reader of ink-print even though it is not a specialized test in the sense of that term as used in this section. The first two passages have been found by the writer to present no special difficulties to such children, the type-face and size being easily legible when the appropriate spectacles or low-vision aids are used. The later passages have also been acceptable to most pupils despite the reduction in print size. For some, however, it may be advisable for these passages to be re-written on a large-face typewriter. In general, the tester must expect to find a sizeable reduction in reading speed, probably of the order of 12–18 months at nine or ten years of age.

The Neale sub-scales are not independent of one another, and the lower levels of performance on the speed and accuracy sub-scales will be associated with an apparent retardation on the comprehension measure, a retardation not attributable to innate ability, poor teaching/learning, or other factors in the child or his environment. In most cases, the testing will be terminated well before the child has reached the limits of his comprehension if the rubric is strictly obeyed. Assessors may therefore be well advised to 'score' the test according to the rubric but to explore the child's competence in more detail by continuing beyond the passage in which the 'error ceiling' is reached. This is done by giving oral corrections of the words mis-pronounced or wrongly identified, and then by giving the comprehension questions provided at the end of the passage. In effect, this turns the later passages of the test into an auditory comprehension exercise, rather than a reading comprehension test. Frequently this will demonstrate that the pupil's comprehension score is on a par with his chronological age despite the fact that his speed and accuracy scores are well below those of his fully sighted age peers. This way of using the test points up more precisely the nature of the educationally handicapping effects of his visual impairment.

Non-specialized tests

When used with partially sighted pupils, the print version of the Neale Analysis of Reading Ability (and its successor, the Neale Analysis of Reading Ability: Revised, 1989) is an example of a non-specialized test. The absence of standardization data for partially sighted readers makes the interpretation of results extremely difficult. Nevertheless, it can be informative for a teacher to know how the partially sighted pupil in her class compares, in terms of, for example, reading speed, with his fully sighted peers. The data obtained from non-specialized tests can alert the teacher, educational psychologist and parent, to the problems certain kinds of activity can cause for the learner who suffers from severe visual impairment. In the integrated setting, it may be all too easy to infer general retardation on the basis of depressed scores in specific areas of functioning. When such scores are set against others that are superior (in areas of functioning where the visual defect is not likely to have handicapping effects), the teacher can be alerted to the need to vary the mode of input. An example of this would be the use of audio-tapes for set texts in English at late secondary school level. The great dearth of adequately standardized tests will in any case oblige assessors to rely upon non-specialized instruments. With growing experience of the unique need and sometimes aberrant course of development of visually handicapped children, the assessor will become more expert in administering, interpreting and deriving useful information from such tests.

British Picture Vocabulary Scale (BPVS)

The BPVS (Dunn *et al.*, 1982) is an individually administered test standardized on a sample of over 3,000 British subjects (the test itself being derived from the well-known American Peabody Picture

Vocabulary Test). It is described as measuring a child's listening vocabulary, and because of its positive correlation with more general measures of intelligence can 'provide some indication of general ability'. Each page contains four line drawings representing objects or events, and the child has to select the picture that corresponds to the single word uttered by the tester. The response can be a nod, a simple pointing gesture or the number of the picture.

Although it was not devised for the visually handicapped (and certainly cannot be used at all with the blind), it has a number of features that can make it informative for teachers of the partially sighted. It is quick and easy to administer. It covers the full school age range (extending downwards to age 2.5 years and upwards to 18 +), at least for the normally sighted population on whom it was standardized. The drawings are decipherable by most partially sighted children, although it is important to ensure that any prescribed or recommended low vision aid is actually used by the child during the testing (alternatively the whole page can be enlarged by means of a closed circuit television magnifier). In addition, informal recording of the way in which the child approaches the task can indicate how he uses his vision (e.g. left-to-right and up-and-down scanning movements; distance at which he needs to be from the page; willingness to suspend his judgement until all four pictures have been examined and re-examined; angle at which the head, or the book, has to be held; the effect of the brightness of the light (and the direction from which it comes); and the attention span for visually presented and visually demanding tasks).

In matters relevant to ordinary classroom conditions, the BPVS can provide some information about visual functioning not available to the teacher from the optometrist's assessment of near vision. However, what cannot be inferred from a poor score on this test is that the child is of below average intelligence. While for normally sighted children it may be legitimate for the test constructors to refer to the high correlation between the BPVS and more general measures of intelligence, this relationship will not necessarily hold good for the partially sighted. The author has evidence from his own investigations that the visual demands of the tasks, or the prior visual experiences of the subject, can lead to quite low scores on tests such as this by children who will obtain very high scores on other, non-visual tests of intelligence. A fuller analysis of the relationship between scores of partially sighted children on the earlier version, viz. the English Picture Vocabulary Test, and other perceptual and intelligence measures can be found in Foster (1973) who reported statistically significant differences between sighted and partially sighted learners in the age range 9.0−10.5 years. Nevertheless, it can be a quick and easy method of obtaining preliminary information about some aspects of a child's perceptual and intellectual capacities, but low scores should not be given the same credence as high scores.

British Ability Scales (BAS)

The BAS (Elliott *et al.*, 1983) is described by its publishers in their catalogue as

> the only complete general cognitive abilities battery developed and standardized in Britain, meeting the requirements of the 1981 Education Act . . . [it] provides a detailed profile of a child's cognitive strengths and weaknesses in up to 23 separate areas . . . [and thus] provides objective evidence and support for decisions about children in need of intervention, special teaching, and care.

It covers the age range 2.5 to 17.5 years and its 23 sub-scales are organized into six process areas:

- Speed of information processing;
- Reasoning;
- Spatial imagery;
- Perceptual matching;
- Short-term memory;
- Retrieval and application of knowledge.

The scales have not been standardized for use with visually handicapped children and since many of the sub-scales contain items and tasks that are presented visually, most of them are unsuitable for blind children. However, two of the Reasoning sub-scales, viz. Similarities and Social reasoning, consist of items that are presented orally and that require an oral response; and this is also the procedure in the Recall of digits sub-scale (testing short-term memory) and the Word definitions sub-scale (retrieval and application of knowledge). These four sub-scales can therefore be administered even to totally blind subjects. Unfortunately, despite their description in the test manual as requiring motor or verbal responses to verbal stimuli, the verbal-tactile matching, the verbal comprehension, and the verbal fluency sub-scales all have, in fact, some visual components in them, thus making them unsuitable for administration to children who cannot see.

In principle, all the sub-scales are applicable to children registered as partially sighted; but considerable caution needs to be exercised in interpreting the results of those sub-scales, e.g. Block design and Recall of designs, where the processes being assessed place great demands upon vision. The 'Power' version of the Block design test has time limits that make it exceedingly difficult for the child with a restricted visual field. Paradoxically, the test that is almost entirely concerned with speed, the Speed of information processing sub-scale, may be of special value in generating information about a partially sighted child's ability to pick up and use visually presented materials. It is so designed that all the items within the scale are easy in the conventional sense, i.e. it is possible for most people to solve them, the main difference among subjects being the time taken. The 'ability scores' obtained from the raw scores provide a measure of the child's performance and can be used as a baseline against which to check future progress.

One section of the sub-scale, designed for the child who has not yet learned to recognize numerals, consists of rows and columns of circles, with each circle having one, two or three small squares inscribed within it. The task for the child is to identify the circle in each row containing the most squares and either point to it or mark it with pencil. Each test item occupies a whole page of the test booklet and one mistake per page is allowable, provided the whole page has been completed within the specified time limits. The later sections of the sub-scale also comprise rows and columns, the requirement here being the identification and marking of the largest number in each row. The items increase in difficulty, with those at the end being made up of five rows and five columns, each row having five five-digit numbers.

For the person of normal sight, the main processes involved include forward and backward scanning, and motivation to complete the task quickly. For the visually handicapped person, the problems may be described as follows:

(1) visual information received by the brain being inaccurate in some way (incomplete or distorted);
(2) difficulties with fixation by the subject, which in turn may lead to fatigue and frustration;
(3) as the amount of information registered by the eye may be restricted, the effort and time to scan and track will be greater, and there will be greater demands on short-term memory capacity;
(4) manipulation of low vision aids of any type will be likely to slow down the speed of gathering information;
(5) performance will depend, to a certain extent, on the amount of formal training the visually handicapped person has received in scanning, in tracking techniques and in efficient use of low vision aids.

A preliminary investigation by Mason and Tobin (1986) showed that while some partially sighted children were able to perform at a very high level on this test, the task constituted, overall, one of considerable difficulty for these severely visually impaired youngsters. While it would not be valid to infer that children registered as partially sighted always perform at a below average level as compared with the fully sighted on a task of this nature, the data presented here do indicate the need for this phenomenon to be investigated in greater depth and with a larger and more representative sample. The British Ability Scales are now being used with large numbers of children of school age and, with the requirement under the 1981 Education Act for children with special needs to be objectively assessed for 'statementing' purposes, it is important that abilities should be measured as accurately as possible. At the very least, the present findings suggest that some able, partially sighted children may not be able to cope with the time demands that this particular test imposes. A wide discrepancy between scores on other BAS sub-scales and the visual information processing sub-scale may provide educationally significant information about the kinds of difficulties such pupils may experience in an integrated setting, especially when following courses leading up to external public examinations.

The fact, too, that there is considerable variation in performance among the partially sighted, with some highly competent children scoring at the 80th and 90th centiles, while the majority is well below average, raises some important questions. Further research is certainly needed to see what, if any, relationship exists between, on the one hand, measured visual acuities and/or the nature of the visual defects (especially degenerative conditions) and, on the other, the ability to scan quickly and accurately in tasks relevant to the classroom. Of equal importance is the regular up-dating of information on pupils' levels of functioning in relation to their peers, so that decisions about placement, about the use of low vision aids, and about additional time allowances in public examinations can be made and set against a background of detailed and reliable evidence. Performance on this particular sub-scale should be helpful to those who have to advise and guide fifteen- to seventeen-year-old students preparing for GCSE and other examinations. The partially sighted twelve-year-old who scores at the 80th or 90th centile on this test is likely to be able to cope adequately with most of the visually presented materials encountered in science and related subjects of the National Curriculum. A child of similar overall intelligence but who is below the 5th centile on this test will need special help and support.

Speed of Information Processing – Tactile Version

A derivative of the BAS Speed of Information sub-scale is to be found in the American Differential Ability Scales (Elliott, 1990). In turn, a specialized tactile form of this scale has been developed in the UK by Hull and Mason (1993). The authors were interested in comparing the times taken by sighted print-readers and educationally blind braille readers in processing information that they believed to be essentially similar, despite the fact that it was to be presented through two different sensory channels. Some 318 subjects, aged between five and seventeen years, were tested in the UK and Ireland.

Among the significant findings were the tactile/print time ratios. The raised line circles and squares took about 'twice as long to read and process in tactile as opposed to visual form, while the brailled numbers, consistently, take approximately three times as long' (ibid., p.22). Equally significant was the relationship between tactual scanning scores and digit span, the obtained correlation co-efficient being 0.5, indicating a strong relationship between performance on the tactual information processing task and short-term memory capacity. There are educational implications here that need to be recognized by teachers and educational psychologists. The first is to do with additional time allowances and the second with general teaching strategies and methods. The longer scanning time for tactually presented information points up the justification for schools seeking extra time for their braille-reading pupils if they are not to be unfairly handicapped in public examinations upon which their future educational and vocational placements may depend. The greater involvement of short-term memory in such tasks suggests (a) that teachers and designers of tactile illustrations should aim to reduce clutter and all but the most essential information in such diagrams so that readers are not having to try to hold too much 'in store' while registering and integrating the data and (b) that teachers should aim to develop in their pupils the most efficient scanning techniques (two-handed reading, smooth left-to-right hand and finger movements, and use of one hand as a marker or reference point while the other searches forward and back as necessary).

Mathematics

In Great Britain, the development of reading tests for the visually handicapped has not been paralleled by work of a similar nature on assessment procedures in the area of mathematics. This may be due to the widely held belief (see, for example, the *Handbook for School Teachers of the Blind*, College of Teachers of the Blind, 1956) that mathematics as such did not present insuperable difficulties for blind pupils. The difficulties that have invited most attention have been concerned with the recording and lay-out of mathematical symbols, computation and graphical representations. These urgent and very practical problems have been discussed at some length by Whittaker (1967), Tooze (1967) and Sims (1967). In the United States, there is an even larger body of literature (research reports, accounts of actual practice, descriptions of technical aids) in which the writers have addressed themselves to the 'technology' of teaching and practising mathematical concepts. It is in the United States, too, that we find public evidence of an interest in methods of assessing achievement in mathematics. Nolan (1959), for example, undertook an analysis of school differences and identification of areas of low achievement in arithmetic computation, and the most searching early study was carried out by Hayes in his unique *Contributions to a Psychology of Blindness* (Hayes, 1941).

As in other areas of achievement testing, there is a tendency for individual schools and teachers to devise their own 'in-house' assessment instruments, whose validity and reliability have never been measured. It is highly likely that those instruments constructed by teachers with long experience of teaching visually handicapped pupils will have satisfactory face validity at least; whether their criterion, content and construct validities are equally satisfactory cannot be determined since no investigations concerning these matters have been reported. One trial of commercially published tests is that undertaken at Birmingham University's Research Centre for the Education of the Visually Handicapped. As part of the Centre's longitudinal study (Tobin, 1979), the subjects were tested with individually administered, modified tactile and large-print versions of Mathematics Attainment Tests 231A and 190A published by the National Foundation for Educational Research in England and Wales. Test 231A was originally standardized on 6,764 normally sighted children in the age range 7.00 to 8.06, i.e. first-year juniors. Test 190A was standardized on 14,231 normally sighted children in the age range 9.06 to 10.05, i.e. third-year juniors. Both these tests include items covering most of the major concept areas normally covered in the first and third years in primary schools in Great Britain, but in so far as schools continue to have different policies as to the timing and placing in the curriculum of these concepts and operations, individual users of the tests will have to be alert to failures that are due solely to those factors rather than to a pupil's slowness or difficulty in understanding the mathematical principles being tested. With these caveats in mind – and the facility to convert the tests into braille and large print – the teachers of junior-school pupils can use these instruments for comparative and diagnostic purposes. It is to be hoped that work will continue in this area to fill in the gaps that exist at primary-school level.

At the secondary-school stage, Clamp (1988) has examined understanding of number operations, fractions, measurement and algebra by eleven- to fifteen-year-old visually handicapped pupils. In the main study, comprising 114 subjects, there were 57 who were blind and 57 who were partially sighted. The tests she selected were taken from the Chelsea Diagnostic Mathematics Tests (see, for example, Hart, 1980), which are now published by NFER-NELSON. To make the tasks feasible for her subjects, Clamp produced large-print and braille versions of the original ink-print documents, and argues on the basis of her experience of administering the test that 'Using the Chelsea Diagnostic Tests on the visually handicapped is a valuable experience for the pupils and their teachers' (ibid., p.201).

General principles in relation to public examinations

It is generally accepted that visually disabled students should have the same entitlement to the National Curriculum as their fully sighted peers. A corollary of this is that their achievement in public examinations should be given the same recognition. Such recognition should not, however, be seen as demanding no changes whatsoever in the conditions under which the examinations are taken. It is incumbent upon parents, teachers and other advisers to ensure that the 'best practices' of the Examination Boards be applied consistently. Among the most important requirements in this public assessment of scholastic achievement are:

(i)   Quality of materials and presentation. This entails:

    (a) for the visually disabled print reader, the use of high-grade paper so that attempted improvements in the weight or boldness of the print, in the quantity and colour of ink used, and in the print size are not vitiated by 'show through' if examination papers are printed on both sides of a page;

    (b) for print and braille readers, that attention is given to the location of diagrams, graphs and other illustrative matter; in some cases, it will be better to have such illustrations in a separate booklet or folder rather than in the middle of the text;

(c) for braille readers, that consistency of labelling and numbering be adhered to; an example would be the adoption of a consistent method of indenting or 'out-denting' of question and section numbers so that the braillist can be helped to find his way quickly around the page.

(ii) Agreement about additional time allowances and the use of amanuenses.

(a) As has been shown, the visually impaired learner, whether print or braille reader, is unable to process ink-print and embossed information as rapidly as the fully sighted person. All Examination Boards are now aware of this and are willing to avoid handicapping such examinees by insisting upon rigid time schedules. It is sometimes possible to negotiate additional 'reading time' allowances for individual students in the light of specific requirements, but 10 to 15 minutes per hour are allowed as a matter of routine. Failure to apply for such allowances can unfairly penalize a candidate; this practice, and the availability of large-print and braille papers, must be seen as a duty expected of the school or institution preparing blind and partially sighted learners for public examinations.

(b) The use of amanuenses (especially for newly blinded students who have not yet mastered the complexities of fully contracted Grade 2 braille nor become fluent readers and writers of it) is also acknowledged by most Examination Boards as a legitimate entitlement. Teachers and advisers must ensure that there are agreed protocols or guidelines as to what the amanuensis may and may not be allowed to do as regards, for example, reading and interpreting diagrams, asking for words to be spelled or for punctuation to be inserted.

(iii) Use of special equipment and typewritten answers.

(a) Most braillists will expect to be allowed to produce their scripts in braille, using standard braille-writing machines which can be noisy and distracting to other examinees. Arrangements need to be made to avoid distracting these candidates. The advent of micro-computer technology permits quieter writing methods and can make possible the production, almost simultaneously if necessary, of braille and print copy. Again, teachers and advisers must seek agreement with the Board about what can be used and under what conditions.

(b) Most blind and partially sighted adolescents are taught keyboard skills and it is surely reasonable for them to be allowed to produce typed rather than hand-written scripts. This entitlement has to be applied for and has implications, yet again, for avoiding the distracting of other candidates.

There are other factors that must be taken into account by those responsible for preparing visually disabled students for nationally recognized qualifications. For example, there is a growing tendency, and not merely in science, geography, economics and technology examination papers, for the use of more tasks that require candidates to examine and interpret diagrams, graphs, charts and maps. It is often possible for the same concepts to be examined in other ways, and the case should therefore be made to the Examination Boards for alternative questions to be set. There is a danger, otherwise, that technology and science may become inaccessible to some students who may have an aptitude for these kinds of subjects.

Modern languages can also present difficulties not encountered by the print reader. Most of them have their own braille systems, with the embossed symbols not representing the same letters or groups of letters as in Standard English Braille. The study, therefore, of original texts in these languages requires the braillist to master a different set of rules and conventions. While the problem may be more challenging at the learning/preparation rather than at the final examination stage, it is not trivial even then, and the extra burden it imposes on the blind learner can be viewed as handicapping him even further.

The move to what may be called age-related scholastic achievement testing is also a handicap for the visually disabled learner. It has been the practice for some time in the special schools at secondary-age level to have a 'Foundation Year' for all or most pupils. They are thus thrown out of step with their age peers in mainstream schools. In addition, the extra processing time needed by them in reading and writing has been traditionally recognized by entering them for public examinations a year later. The inception of rigid, age-related attainment testing is inimical to their development and their ability to realize their full potential. Its inappropriateness needs to be exposed. Fortunately, the Royal National Institute for the Blind and the Association for the Education and Welfare of the Visually Handicapped have well-established curriculum working parties that can, and do, address these problems on behalf of the pupils, their teachers and their parents. They constitute a mechanism that should be used to ensure that the blind and partially sighted learner is not handicapped twice over.

CHAPTER 5

Visually Impaired Children with Additional Disabilities

The survey by the Royal National Institute for the Blind (RNIB) of blind and partially sighted children in Britain (Walker, *et al.*, 1992) estimates that 56 per cent have at least one other permanent illness or disability. That this may be an underestimate is suggested by Bone and Meltzer (1989) in their survey of the prevalence of disability among children; this enquiry by the Office of Population Censuses and Surveys (OPCS) was not, as the RNIB survey was, based solely upon children identified by the local education authorities (LEAs), and in exploring the prevalence of all disabilities it found that among its sub-group of visually impaired subjects, some 83 per cent had an additional disability. The discrepancy between the RNIB and OPCS estimates is not easily explicable, but one possibility is that the LEAs did not provide the RNIB researchers with information about children whose other disabilities were so severe that the visual impairment was not regarded as of primary significance. Whatever the explanation, it is clear that blindness and partial sight are now most often associated with other serious congenital conditions that can interfere with normal development and learning.

The most frequently reported additional handicapping conditions in the RNIB survey were speech, physical and mental disabilities, each of which affected about one-quarter of the sample. Behaviour/social problems and hearing difficulties were each found in nearly one-fifth of the group. Twenty-nine per cent of the subjects had one or two other disabilities and 27 per cent had three or more. What is also of significance is that the prevalence of other disabilities was higher among those children with lower levels of residual vision.

The mere citing of these statistical summaries brings out the heterogeneity of the group of children conventionally labelled as multi-handicapped visually impaired (MHVI). In addressing the task of assessing the MHVI child, Langley (1986) has pointed out that an individual student is as unique as the battery of assessment instruments and processes will need to be (ibid., p.253), thus underlining the importance of an approach that does not rely upon a single test, however well-standardized and however well-buttressed in terms of validity and reliability. The diversity of skills that need to be examined cannot be encompassed in any one instrument, and the assessor should ideally be part of a multi-disciplinary team where there is input from paediatrics, ophthalmology, ophthalmics, psychology, special education and physiotherapy. Allied to this is the acceptance that assessment cannot be a 'one-off' undertaking. Many of the impairments suffered by these children affect cognitive, perceptual and social functioning in quite debilitating ways as metabolic and physiological processes change throughout the course of the day, the week and the month. Diabetes and epilepsy, for example, are just two of the frequently occurring chronic conditions that can have dramatic effects upon sensory and intellectual functioning. Tactual and attentive behaviours are sensitive to variations in the intensity of these conditions, and therefore tasks depending upon these behaviours may be incapable of being carried out on a specific occasion. Obtaining estimates of optimal functioning entails, as a consequence, detailed observations and measurements over a period of days and weeks to take account of such influences.

This wide diversity of competences and needs among such a relatively small group of children has made the development of standardized tests extremely difficult. Quite properly, therefore, the objective has been to provide carers with a means to measure progress rather than to compare the child with his age peers. Even then, the increments of advance and improvement may be so small and their initial occurrence so fleeting that it requires great care in defining in behavioural and operational terms the criteria to be used for recognizing their existence. Failure to be precise will cast doubts on the objectivity and consistency of the observers/assessors.

This can be illustrated by reference to the development of fine motor skills required for fixing square and triangular wooden shapes into a formboard. The MHVI three year old's progress on a task of this nature may be punctuated by apparent regressions from occasional perfect achievement to seemingly aimless moving around of the shapes. What constitutes success in these circumstances? A similar difficulty arises in socialization. Facing the person with whom the child is interacting is observed regularly in 'normal' blind children before the age of five years. It is generally regarded as an indicator of the child's understanding of social relationships and conventions, but how precise does the bodily orientation have to be before this 'item' in the test is passed as correct, especially by a child with significant physical disabilities?

Both these pieces of behaviour fit into the criterion-referenced approach to assessment. Here the concern is not with the extent to which a child conforms to achievement levels found to be typical of his age group but rather with whether or not he can carry out a specific task, like pulling his arm up so that he can be helped to put it into the sleeve of his shirt or coat, or using a spoon to feed himself without excessive spillage. These small changes in competence may be of practical significance to the carer but they rarely constitute pass/fail items in a standardized test. It is in these circumstances that Langley's comments (1986) on the uniqueness of the MHVI pupil and of the procedures for assessing his needs are to be seen as valid, and it is against this background that we understand why individual teachers and institutions have felt obliged to construct their own checklists and observational methods of assessing needs and progress. The purpose has been, as Aitken and Buultjens describe it in their working definition of the use of assessment, to derive 'practical information in order to help bring about beneficial change' (1992, p.14). Best and Bell (1984) have also drawn attention to this training-oriented feature of many of the assessment and observational schedules, both the commercially produced and in the 'in-house' procedures.

The value of 'in-house' procedures, especially when all staff have been involved in their development and trained in their administration, cannot be overstated. As will be argued in due course, it is essential that teachers and care staff do make their own records of each MHVI pupil's overall achievements and of the subsidiary or prerequisite skills. Various kinds of formal observational methods designed by psychologists will be suggested as ways of making these assessments more objective (i.e. open to verification of their consistency when used by different observers), while at the same time being a means for planning teaching programmes.

Tests, checklists and schedules commercially available or in the public domain

In Chapter 3, a description was given of three inventories that were constructed for use with pre-school children. All three (the Maxfield–Buchholz, the Reynell–Zinkin and Oregon Project schemes) can be recommended to be included in the battery of instruments to be assembled by teachers working with the MHVI child. They all focus upon important and universal aspects of motor, cognitive, perceptual and social development, and one of them, the Reynell – Zinkin Scales, contains a sub-scale, entitled Communication, constructed 'as a guide for teaching children who may have combined visual and auditory handicaps' or 'who are not developing verbal language for any other reason, such as severe cerebral palsy' (Reynell, 1979, p.45). The three inventories are perhaps best to be regarded as giving a general framework for thinking about the development of the MHVI child, and for generating hypotheses that can be tested with other more finely detailed measuring instruments.

Something of their inadequacy as assessment schedules for staff working with profoundly multiply handicapped children can be appreciated by examination of particular test items. For example, item 9 of the Exploration of environment sub-scale in the Reynell – Zinkin Scales requires the child to demonstrate directed, purposeful locomotion, with successful, adaptive use of furniture. This achievement typically occurs between 2.5 and 3 years of age with blind children having no additional disabilities, and before 18 months of age among their sighted counterparts. A piece of behaviour that would denote success on this item is 'finding his chair and seating himself at the table for a meal' (ibid., p.40). The paraplegic deaf-blind ten year old may never be able to do this, nor indeed any of the other behaviours suggested as indicating directed, purposeful locomotion 'without adult assistance'. Some of the skills demanded by these three instruments are therefore inappropriate for the MHVI child.

The Oregon Project for Visually Impaired and Blind Pre-school Children (see Chapter 3) had its origins in a home-teaching scheme developed in the United States and now widely known as the Portage materials, the Portage checklist and the Portage Project. In the UK, the publishers of the various packages are NFER-NELSON. The scheme has proliferated a checklist, a classroom curriculum, a parent's guide to early education, an activity chart and a developmental profile, the main components being contained in the British Portage Early Education Programme (see, for example, White and Cameron, 1988). Kiernan (1987, p.169) has argued 'the checklist is also a relatively unimportant part of the package', the teaching suggestions and the whole Portage system/philosophy being the crucial parts of the whole project. The value of the Oregon and Portage approach lies therefore in its design as a means to enable parents, teachers and other care-givers to participate in the business of helping developmentally delayed pre-schoolers to progress from one stage of competence to the next. In acknowledging the value of the Oregon and Portage schemes for home and classroom training purposes, and especially for their emphasis on designing methods for improving each of the skills identified as defective by the checklist, there still remain doubts about the make-up and size of the sample of visually impaired children selected for the field testing and about the locating of some of the items in the age range pinpointed for them by the Oregon Project workers.

This is not merely a technical quibble; parents and their care-givers can be made anxious if, for example, before one year of age the totally blind child is not holding out his arms and legs while being dressed, a behaviour signalled in the Oregon checklist as to be expected at this age. Socialization can also be delayed, especially with regard to imitating the actions of adults and other children where vision is such a powerful triggering device and where visual interaction can be so powerfully reinforcing. The MHVI child will almost certainly be at an even greater disadvantage, with quite minor deficits in hearing and motor development serving to exacerbate the handicaps arising directly from the visual disabilities. Kiernan is undoubtedly right to play down the importance of the checklist in the Portage, and by implication in the Oregon, and yet it is the checklist that initially guides the assessor and the parent in their observations.

Another criterion-referenced test is the BAB, the Behaviour Assessment Battery (Kiernan and Jones, 1982) and although it was not designed with MHVI children in mind, its broad coverage of early cognitive (including language), social and perceptual skills makes it a useful tool for teachers with experience and a good understanding of the problems of these children. Many of the sub-sections of the test explore the child's visual tracking, inspection and scanning behaviours, and can thus be helpful in assessing whether and how he makes use of any residual sight. The authors have not included teaching suggestions within the Battery but the theoretical and empirical framework upon which it was built makes the BAB very decidedly teaching and training oriented, as can be inferred from its use of prompting and reinforcement procedures to encourage the child to respond during the administration of the test.

A procedure that overtly espouses a combined assessment and training model is *The Next Step on the Ladder* (Simon, 1986). Its instructional and criterion-referenced approach is brought out in the statement of the general aims (ibid., p.12), viz. to 'obtain an indication of the child's current level of function in each area of development, for the purpose of deciding upon the most appropriate programme of training for that child'. The core of the assessment and training methodology was developed in the Deaf/Blind Unit at Lea Hospital, Bromsgrove, where the editor, Professor G.B. Simon, was the Medical Director. Over many years, the multi-disciplinary team assembled by Gerry Simon pioneered new testing and instructional techniques for children with multiple handicaps, and particularly those with visual and hearing impairments. The outcome of this painstaking work is a Developmental Assessment Scale and a set of recommendations for parents and others to encourage looking and listening, movement, manual dexterity (fine movements and co-ordinated use of the hands), social development, self-help skills, and communication (signs, gestures and speech).

The training methods are based on behavioural principles, starting from detailed observation of existing levels of performance and skills, and then giving immediate reinforcement to each step or behaviour related to the specified goal. For example, if the goal is to enable the child to sit up or stand, a pre-requisite achievement is complete head control, the attainment of which is then followed by helping him to pull himself up from a supine position with the head moving in line with the body. Each movement by the child that is in the desired direction is rewarded, with support being gradually withdrawn and with increasing demands being made upon the child. An important component in the observation, assessment and teaching processes is the identification of the reinforcers – bodily contact, food, vibration, light, textured materials, sounds – that are uniquely effective for the child at that time.

Best and Bell (1984) in their analysis of twelve schedules for the profoundly handicapped have argued that there is 'no single assessment instrument' possessing 'all the characteristics to measure every aspect of development adequately'. In listing *The Next Step on the Ladder*, these two commentators draw attention to its value for the MHVI child on account of its specific concern with the use of any residual sight. The visual behaviours assessed are very basic indeed, starting with noting whether the child will turn his head towards a light source at a distance of about six inches, the observer then moving the light further away for recording when interest starts and finishes. *The Next Step on the Ladder* has the added merit that it can be used with very young visually impaired children where there is no suspicion of other disabilities. Its criterion-referenced orientation pre-supposes that the tasks, and their successful achievement, have not been selected solely on the basis of age norms and developmental ages. In some sections of the Assessment Scale, there is a clear hierarchical ordering – climbing stairs being located after such obviously prerequisite actions as sitting, crawling, standing and walking. To that extent, therefore, there is an acknowledgement that chronological age has some relation to the emergence of specific competencies. The assessor familiar with norm-referenced developmental schedules will recognize in some sections the dependence of the orderings of behaviours and skills upon well-established developmental checklists. The test constructors have nevertheless avoided all reference to age-related norms, requiring the users to focus upon manifestly important skills, their components and precursors, and crucially upon methods to facilitate their acquisition and maintenance. The other requirement – the multi-disciplinary team – is based on the belief that 'no single person or profession can ever hope to possess all the skills necessary' for the adequate assessment of these children's problems (Simon, 1986, pp.12–13).

One commentator, Holmes (1992), has criticized the instrument because of lack of information 'about the development of this scale, or a rationale for why items were selected' (ibid., p.93), and because it has not been standardized and no data are available as to reliability. Holmes does go on nevertheless to praise the accompanying manual for its clarity and precision, seeing these qualities as essential when untrained staff are to be part of the team carrying out the assessment.

The most recent research-based system that combines assessment and teaching is *Vision for Doing. Assessing Functional Vision of Learners who are Multiply Disabled* (Aitken and Buultjens, 1992). The authors have set themselves the task of making explicit the 'links between assessment findings and suggestions as to what might be carried out with the learner' on the basis of the observations. The title of the manual does not bring out the wide range of behaviours being assessed. There are 17 sections, four of them dealing directly with non-visual senses, encompassing: responses to sound, the learner's sense of touch, the learner's sense of smell and the sense of taste. This attention to the non-visual modalities makes the instrument much more useful than the title would suggest. Another of its merits on the training side is its willingness to acknowledge that different theories of teaching and learning can be relevant to solving some of the problems that these children pose. Behaviour modification may be appropriate for treating some mannerisms (eye-poking, rocking, for example) but other approaches are also recommended, the requirement being that care-givers should first of all record instances of the behaviour to determine whether there is a pattern that becomes apparent over a prolonged period of observation. The recording of the behaviour may, according to the authors, give rise to other teaching procedures – facilitating substitute activities, involving the learner in other motivating behaviour or verbal commands.

Another characteristic of the Aitken and Buultjens approach is that it attempts to avoid both a medical classification of the child and his difficulties and an educational categorization based upon such groupings as profoundly handicapped, severe learning difficulties or deaf-blind. Instead, the starting point is the 'learner's ability to do things' (ibid., p.39). What this means is that the initial interest is in how the child responds to objects and events in his immediate surroundings: from this baseline systematic methods of intervention are then planned. An example of this can be seen in Section 16, Visual Responses to People, where observing that a child does not respond to faces but does so to reflective surfaces, such as spectacles, can suggest the linking of the positive response to something that the child likes, e.g. being tickled. The simple recommendation is 'As soon as the child looks at the glasses, tickle him. Then remove your glasses. After a time, tickle him while he is looking in that direction, even though no glasses may be worn at that time' (ibid., p.216). The use of these behaviourist techniques brings out again the authors' willingness to adopt whatever teaching/learning theories and methods seem most appropriate for a particular goal for a particular child.

The emphasis upon what the child can do is reflected in the structure of the Summary chart (see Figure 5.1) which provides a profile of an individual's achievements in each of the 17 assessment areas. The chart is also to be used for showing: a general level for the assessor's/teacher's intervention, the limit of the learner's visual abilities and thirdly the optimum sense around which the intervention is to be concentrated. This latest addition to the list of assessment schedules is undoubtedly one of the most precisely focused. Its concern with behaviours and skills related to home and classroom activities makes it an invaluable tool for the specialist teacher and the non-specialist who may have an MHVI child placed in her charge.

The Profile of Adaptive Skills (Stockley and Richardson, 1991) is a relatively new rating scale 'developed in response to the need for a profile which would take account of the personal and social development of older adolescents and young adults with special needs' (ibid., p.3). The authors of this scale have referred to the disadvantage arising from the fact that many tests are restricted in the sense that their

Figure 5.1 Section 18 summary chart

Section Number	Assessment Area		*Aware*	*Attend*	*Localize*	*Recognize*	*Under-stand*
Section 1	The Learner		▒	▒	▒	▒	▒
Section 2	Background information						
Section 3	Observing the Learner						▒
Section 4	Responses to Sound						
Section 5	Sense of Touch						
Section 6	Sense of Smell				▒		
Section 7	Sense of Taste				▒		
Section 8	Observing Learner's Eye		▒	▒	▒	▒	▒
Section 9	Responses to Light				▒	▒	▒
Section 10	Reflected Light				▒	▒	▒
Section 11	Approaching Object					▒	▒
Section 12	Movement	Horizontal			▒	▒	▒
		Vertical			▒	▒	▒
		Circular				▒	▒
Section 13	Visual Fields	Upper half			▒	▒	▒
		Lower half			▒	▒	▒
		Preferences				▒	▒
Section 14	Contrast	High		▒	▒	▒	▒
		Medium			▒	▒	▒
		Low				▒	▒
Section 15	Size	Large		▒	▒	▒	▒
		Medium			▒	▒	▒
		Small				▒	▒
Section 16	People						▒
Section 17	Mobility						▒

▒ The filled area indicates that it is not possible to obtain this information from the assessment alone.

Source: Aitken and Buultjens (1992).

administration and interpretation require a psychologist trained for this purpose. The Profile of Adaptive Skills has been designed for use by anyone 'who has care of a student'. Although no formal standardization data are provided in the test manual, the validity of the scale rests upon the authors' own experience of its genesis and use in a residential college of further education specializing in the teaching of visually handicapped students with moderate to severe learning difficulties.

The areas of functioning covered by the scale are: academic skills (communication, literacy, numeracy); vocational skills; living and independence skills; social skills; and mobility skills. Completion of the Profile is effected by rating each skill/behaviour under the headings Unable (student cannot perform the task or understand the concept), Assisted (student requires help for most of the time), Inconsistent (student can usually complete the task unaided but may need assistance from time to time) and Competent (student can perform the task wholly unaided at all times). It is assumed that assessments will be repeated, thus allowing for measurement of progress.

This scale is a most useful addition to the assessment battery, wide-ranging in its coverage of educationally and socially important skills, with the Profile itself being a potentially instructive document for the student and for handing on to other instructors and care-givers responsible for his well-being.

There are other commercially produced assessment procedures that have been developed in the United States of America, and although their use in the UK is not yet widespread, they can offer valuable insights to assessors-practitioners, complementing the more readily accessible instruments that have been examined above. Figure 5.2 lists and describes four of these procedures.

Arising from a series of investigations undertaken at Condover Hall School for Blind Children with Other Handicaps and especially within the unit for deaf-blind pupils, known as Pathways, Tobin and Myers (1978) reported the development of methods for assessing aspects of short-term memory capacity in children suffering from severe visual and hearing impairment. Of course, most conventional tests of intelligence contain items that require the exercise of what is often called 'short-term memory'. They typically consist of sequences of digits or letters, but the content may take a variety of forms, all, however, requiring the subject to perceive, encode, store, recall and reproduce the original information. Tasks like this have been built into the tests devised by van Dijk (1971) and into the video-tape evaluation system developed in the United States and described by Donlon and Curtis (1972). Among the

Figure 5.2 Four assessment procedures for MHVI children, developed and published in the United States of America

Test/Schedule/Checklist	Behaviours/Skills Covered
1. *Ordinal Scales of Psychological Development.* Uzgiris,I. and Hunt, J.M. Published by the University of Illinois Press, 1975. Latest edition, 1980. Useful reference: Dunst, C. (1980) *A Clinical and Educational Manual for use with the Uzgiris and Hunt Scales of Infant Psychological Development.* Austin, Texas: PRO-ED.	Originally developed for use with non-handicapped children up to age two years but latest edition has many items appropriate for developmentally delayed children of all ages, but some sub-scales require too much vision for severely visually impaired and all blind children. Based upon Piagetian model of development.
2. *Behaviour Rating Instrument for Autistic and Other Atypical Children.* Ruttenberg, B.A., Kalish, B.I., Wenar, C. and Wolf, E.G. Chicago: Stoelting, 1977. Useful reference: Schein, J.D., Kates, L., Wolf, E.G. and Theil, L. (1983). 'Assessing and developing the communication abilities of deaf-blind children.' *Journal of Visual Impairment and Blindness* 77, 4, 152−7.	The BRIAAC is an observational schedule for measuring skills and behaviours at very low levels of development. As a means of assessing deaf-blind children's communication abilities, it needs to be associated with AIM (Assessment-Intervention Model for Deaf-Blind Students) as described in the Schein *et al.* paper.
3. *Callier-Azusa Scale-H: Cognition and Communication.* University of Texas, Dallas, 1983. Useful reference: Stillman, R.D. and Battle, C.W. 'Developmental assessment of communicative abilities in the deaf-blind'. In: Ellis, D. (ed.) *Sensory Impairments in Mentally Handicapped People.* London: Croom Helm, 1986.	One of the few scales designed for deaf-blind children. Assessment is by direct observation of the subjects in their normal environments (home, classroom), and the major areas of interest are representational and symbolic activities, receptive communication, intentional communication and reciprocity (participation in reciprocal communications and interactions).
4. *Functional Vision Inventory for the Multiple and Severely Handicapped.* Langley, M.B. Chicago: Stoelting, 1980. Useful reference: Sebba, J. (1988). 'A system for assessment and intervention for pre-school profoundly retarded multiply handicapped children'. M.Ed. Thesis, University of Manchester, England.	A procedure for observing and recording visual responses, including integration of vision and cognitive and motor processing, using available materials in the classroom. No explicit training suggestions but the information elicited can in fact be used for some teaching/learning activities. The British adaptation, by Sebba, explores differential tracking responses in sitting and supine positions.

claims made for including these tests of immediate memory in intelligence tests are that they provide data about the subject's ability to attend and concentrate and that they are, at least in children, correlated with what might be termed 'general intelligence'. There is, too, a developmental aspect since it has been found that memory span increases steadily in step with age until early adolescence when it reaches its maximum. As regards the attention/concentration claim, there is a mass of research literature demonstrating how easy it is to impair encoding and recall by various kinds of distractions, and it might be expected therefore that the child with sensory deficits would be at a serious disadvantage. He is severely disabled by the inadequacy of his senses when it comes to the picking up and transmission of the data into his memory 'store', and he is liable to suffer interference from other internal and external stimuli during the relatively more extended period of time when he is re-transmitting the data. The attention/concentration capacity of the deaf-blind child is in that sense much more vulnerable to disruption.

Evidence and arguments of this kind would constitute a sufficient justification in themselves for attempting to devise purpose-built measures of memory span in children whose sensory impairments make the usual vision and auditory tests inappropriate. The positive, if small, correlation with overall intellectual functioning would, in the current absence of any instrument for measuring such intelligence, be reason enough for welcoming the appearance of valid memory tests. A more potent reason however can be adduced: most human communication systems require some sort of temporal sequencing of the information. Speech puts phonemes and words into a time sequence; writing arranges graphemes and words in a spatial sequence which is perceived over time. These, and other, systems necessitate at the receiver's end the perception and storing, and then the integrating of the stored information into meaningful wholes. In all of them, there is the exercise of short-term memory processes. The demands on immediate memory are probably even greater in the various communication systems now in use with the deaf-blind. Finger-spelling may be done with great speed and fluency by the experts but it is inevitable that any system entailing the signalling of every letter by means of a physical movement and pressure will be relatively slow, and thus involve the 'receiver' in holding information in store until enough has been received to permit 'closure'; that is, recognition of the whole word or phrase. The capacity of the memory store will therefore be a significant factor in determining the child's ability not only to master but to use such a code for transmitting and receiving messages. Superimposed upon his defective sensory system is a mode of communication that by its very nature will require intelligence, concentration and maximal use of the available storage space in the user.

The tests designed and validated by these investigators (an example is shown in Figure 5.3) are a body touch test, a removed object test and a finger touch test, and they are now all in the public domain. That is, they can be used, free of charge, by teachers and psychologists who are attempting to get some measure of the deaf-blind child's ability to receive, register and retrieve information presented in a sequential manner. The materials used are easy to assemble and are described in sufficient detail in the report (Tobin and Myers, 1978) to enable potential users to prepare their own versions of the tests. The questions

Figure 5.3 Finger Touch Test. Score sheet (see Tobin and Myers, 1978)

Child's Name _____ Date of Birth _____ Date of Test _____

School _____

Visual Acuity (best, corrected vision) _____

Degree of Hearing Loss _____

Favoured Hand (underline) _____ Left/Right _____

Practice Items

4 3 2 1   Score

(i)	T,	..	..	..	..	____
(ii)	2,	..	..	..	..	____
(iii)	3,	1,	..	..	..	____
(iv)	4,	2,	..	..	..	____

Main Test

Score

Item										Score
Item 1	4,	..	..	..	..	..	..	..	..	____
Item 2	1,	..	..	..	..	..	..	..	..	____
Item 3	T,	3,	..	..	..	..	..	..	..	____
Item 4	2,	4,	..	..	..	..	..	..	..	____
Item 5	1,	T,	3,	..	..	..	..	..	..	____
Item 6	4,	1,	4,	..	..	..	..	..	..	____
Item 7	T,	2,	2,	3,	..	..	..	..	..	____
Item 8	4,	1,	3,	3,	..	..	..	..	..	____
Item 9	T,	4,	4,	2,	1,	..	..	..	..	____
Item 10	3,	1,	2,	2,	T,	..	..	..	..	____
Item 11	4,	3,	T,	1,	T,	3,	..	..	..	____
Item 12	T,	1,	2,	T,	4,	1,	..	..	..	____
Item 13	2,	2,	4,	T,	1,	1,	T,	..	..	____
Item 14	T,	4,	2,	T,	T,	1,	3,	..	..	..

TOTAL SCORE [   ]

Maximum score   56

of validity and reliability are discussed at some length in the report, and the researchers argue that the tests afford opportunity for the systematic observation of deaf-blind children, and yield information that could be of value to those concerned with teaching communication and other skills.

Observational methods of assessment

Informal methods

While attention has been given to various kinds of formal and clinical methods of assessment — sometimes by means of standardized tests giving rise to numerical scores — the potential value of formal and informal observation has also been mentioned. The properly validated test enables the user to focus upon specific skills, to compare one child with another, and in some cases to obtain a 'profile' of him in related areas of functioning. There are still many dimensions of human behaviour, however, that have not been analysed and described in terms of the discrete elements of which they are constituted and by which they can be measured. (Some would also argue that there are aspects of behaviour that cannot usefully be thought of as being arranged on a scale to which numbers can be attached.) It is in relation to these behaviours that observational methods may be appropriate. The existence of these attributes must be detectable in some way if the observer is to convince other people that she can recognize their presence and infer something about their effect upon the attitudes, actions and capabilities of the person being assessed. It has been argued earlier that those experienced in assessment procedures develop a kind of internal checklist against which they 'measure' these characteristics, and they are alert to the potential significance of apparently covert actions, styles of behaviour, and methods and strategies of responding and interacting.

If we label these kinds of assessment as 'informal' and thus differentiate them from objective tests with their standardized scores or their criterion-referenced hierarchy of skills and all that is subsumed under the notion of objective validation, it is nevertheless still possible to arrange them on a scale. At one end are the 'checklist' procedures. These may be exemplified by the careful noting of whether the subject seeks regular verbal or non-verbal reinforcement or reward during the interaction; of the extent to which he uses any residual vision for finding objects or monitoring his own hand movements; of the presence and frequency of mannerisms (rocking, eye-poking, etc.) and of the events that initiate or inhibit manneristic behaviour; of distractibility (whether caused by the presence of other people, of extraneous sounds or the increasing difficulty of the tasks being attempted); and of the presence of other handicaps, such as slight spasticity in one hand, that might affect performance on certain items of the standardized test. The other end of the scale or continuum might best be described as a general alertness, awareness or sensitivity on the part of the tester that facilitates the registering of nuances of verbal and non-verbal behaviour, of attitudes and of other personality characteristics that are difficult to anticipate and describe but that can nevertheless be perceived by the practised observer, and that may help to 'explain' some aspects of performance on the test. The tester who fails to cultivate such informal observational skills will obtain little more from the assessment session than a number, a quotient; in other words, little more than is obtained from and by an automatic weighing machine.

This harsh analogy is no mere figure of speech: the insensitive tester, unlike the weighing machine, can actually affect the subject's performance. The establishment of rapport helps to put the subject at ease and thus elicit his highest level of functioning; the observant tester is better able to effect this rapport since in noting how the subject behaves she is noting also what brings about the necessary combination of relaxation and motivation. Informal, observational methods are therefore an essential part of the assessment process, and should never be seen as separate from, or antagonistic to, objective testing.

Human behaviour is a complex phenomenon and in isolating specific segments of it, as in attempting to evaluate mathematical and reading skills, we are making many assumptions about what something is and how important it is. Many of these assumptions are never made explicit. If this is the case with widely used, well-validated tests, then it is even more likely that we shall overlook the prejudices and preconceptions operating when we make inferences from the relatively unstructured observations associated with informal methods. It is for this reason that, in pressing for the recognition of the value of such methods, we must not overstate the case that can be made for them. They are, nevertheless, well-suited to the conditions and constraints of the classroom and their use will accord easily with the predilections of teachers whose training and attitudes are oriented towards the recognition of individual differences rather than general normative trends.

78

Formal methods

Within the field of child psychology, there is also a range of formal observational methods that are highly objective, in the sense that their use by different observers will produce the same, or very nearly the same, record of what occurred. They differ from the informal procedures in a number of ways, principally in that they are pre-planned: the child or the behaviour, or the time, or the place, or all four are specified in advance and a set method of recording is prepared. To this extent, they have much in common with standardized tests. They differ from such tests, however, in that they are not based upon notions of normal standards of what can be expected by children of such and such an age, and they do not consist of a set of items that are checked as right or wrong. They are essentially procedures for observing and recording activities and behaviours of interest and concern to the teacher.

'Event sampling' is one such procedure, the practice being to select some behaviour, such as eye-poking or rocking or vocalization, that is of interest and then to record all instances of it with a view to determining its nature, its frequency and possibly the circumstances that induce or inhibit its emergence.

'Time sampling' is another and involves observing a child or a group of children, recording selected, or all, behaviours occurring during definite short periods of time (10 to 15 minutes usually), the observation periods being spaced to suit the interests and intentions of the observer. An advantage of this observational technique is that it allows comparisons to be made as between individuals, and for the same individual in different settings and at different times.

A quasi-experimental approach can be adopted by altering the settings or the conditions, with time and event sampling procedures being used for observing and recording, with a view to estimating the effects of specific independent variables.

'Diary' records are among the oldest of all methods of systematically recording human behaviour. All, or selected, activities manifested by the subject can be noted in such records on a daily or weekly basis. They are susceptible to bias in that the writing up of the diary can be influenced by the vagaries of the observer's memory and her re-ordering or re-interpreting of events.

These methods, especially time and event sampling, require the preparation of 'protocols', that is, record sheets divided into rows and columns corresponding to time intervals and behaviour categories so that the recording can consist of merely a tick or other mark showing the occurrence of an item of behaviour. With portable tape-recorders and video-recorders, an extra dimension of speed, accuracy and rechecking can be built into the system, thus improving its objectivity. The use of 'hardware' is, of course, easier in a clinic where a team assessment approach is in operation, and where fellow professionals can re-hear or re-watch the child again and again.

While these more formal methods of observation may not be easy to set up in the classroom, they can be so informative as to warrant some reasonable expenditure of time, energy and preparation. With the disruptive or distractible child, they may be the only way in which to investigate precipitating or causative factors. They thus pinpoint the independent variables and can help to generate hypotheses about remedial treatments that can then be put to the test.

An example of the use of observational methods is taken from Tobin *et al.* (1972) where the topic of interest was the eye-poking manneristic behaviour of children in an experimental and educational unit for visually handicapped and mentally retarded children.

One investigation entailed observation of a four-year-old, non-ambulant boy for whom VOMs (visually oriented mannerisms) were a major pre-occupation. He was observed between 9.00 a.m. and 4.00 p.m. each day for five days to obtain some initial information on the kind and frequency of the eye-mannerisms, and then detailed recording continued for a further 10 days, each recording session lasting 10 minutes, with sessions spaced throughout the day to obtain mean frequencies for each of the hours between 9.00 a.m. and 4.00 p.m. In Figure 5.4, the mean per 10-minute period for each hour is presented

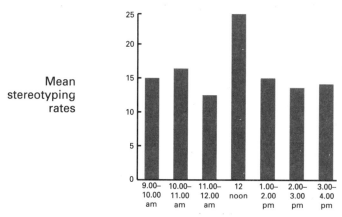

Figure 5.4 Mean rates of VOM's per 10-minute block (one subject – non-ambulant)

graphically. During the day the rate of manneristic behaviour was fairly constant, except during the hour when the children were being given their midday meal which was taken with the children seated around tables in groups of five or six. Although the child under observation did not feed himself, his supervisor was trying to teach him to hold the spoon himself. The increase in VOMs may be due to extra stress caused by the new demands being made upon him.

Some support for this interpretation, vague and ill-defined though the term 'stress' may be, is perhaps to be found in the pattern of results obtained with the same subject when he was restrained in various other ways. Observation of frequency of VOMs when he was placed in a rocker, a toy from which he could not move unaided, showed a mean rate of 18 per 10-minute period as compared with a mean of 13.3 per 10-minute period when he was left to lie prone on the floor. A similar increase was recorded when he was released after a 5-minute period of 'walking practice'. The mean pre-walking rate was 1.4 VOMs per minute as compared with 2.1 per minute after the practice session. The child did not like the exercise, and the increase in mannerisms may thus be positively correlated with induced stress.

For comparison, four other subjects − all noted for fairly high rates of VOMs − were observed. Recording was carried out in 10-minute periods randomly arranged throughout the day over a period of ten days; in addition, mannerisms were recorded for each child for a period of 10 minutes during each lunch-hour session. In three cases, the means were lower for the meal-time period (6.5/2.5, 9.7/9.0 and 5.2/3.5), and higher in one other (0.75/3.0). If the stress theory was correct for the previous subject, it must be inferred that meal-time was not a stressful time for the first three of these new subjects but might be so for subject number four.

That the stress theory is not the complete answer is shown by another series of observations in which four ambulant subjects were observed sitting, standing, crawling and walking in the playroom and in the ward-pool. Behaviour was recorded for each child for periods of one minute, sub-divided into five-second units, at intervals throughout the day. The mean numbers of VOMs averaged over the four children for the period of the observations were: sitting, 3.5 per minute; standing, 4.1 per minute; crawling, 1.25 per minute; walking, 1.25 per minute. The inverse relationship between gross motoric activity and rate of stereotyping seems clear enough. These findings fit Guess's (1967) explanation that 'stimuli encouraging motoric responses provide more effective alternative activities' and thus reduce the rate of stereotyping among visually handicapped retardates.

In another series of observations on possible determinants of the VOMs, recordings were made of the numbers of children displaying these mannerisms under different lighting conditions within the playroom. Casual observation had suggested that there was a tendency for children to be drawn towards a french-window (other windows in the room being rather high). Some, of course, were not able to choose a preferred spot since they were non-ambulant. Observation consisted of recording, for a period of one week on three occasions each day, (i) the number of children positioned near the window, (ii) their behaviour and (iii) the number of those who were facing the light source. In Table 5.1, details are given of numbers and percentages of children indulging in manneristic activities under different conditions of external illumination. Although only one-fifth of all subjects were classified as being drawn towards the french-window, over half (57 per cent) of this sub-group were observed to be occupied with mannerisms of this kind. More children were seen to be drawn to the light-source under bright than under dull conditions. The inferences would be that light attracts the children and that it acts as a stimulus for visually oriented behaviour.

From these investigations it would seem that manneristic behaviour centred on the eyes may often be increased under conditions of stress and in the presence of higher levels of illumination, and may be decreased as a consequence of behaviours involving gross motoric activity. The presence of such mannerisms under many different conditions suggests, however, that they are not tied to any specified stimulus. They would seem to be both a source of self-stimulation and a response to increased intensity of certain kinds of external stimulation. Their widely generalized causation makes control and elimination more difficult. In so far as they replace other, more productive activities, they

Table 5.1 Details of VOM behaviour under different conditions of light

A.	Children facing light.	=	44 (20% of grand total)
B.	Percentage of (A) indulging in VOMs.	=	57% (11% of grand total)
C.	Children NOT facing light but indulging in VOMs.	=	9 (4% of grand total)
D.	Average number of children observed facing light in bright conditions.	=	4.7
E.	Average number of children observed facing light in dull conditions.	=	2.0
F.	Average number facing light and indulging in VOMs when bright.	=	2.0
G.	Average number facing light and indulging in VOMs when dull.	=	1.3

are seen as undesirable. They can, however, be reduced at any given time by substituting tasks that need the use of greater physical force (small objects are inadequate since they are used for eye-poking, etc.). It may also be that more uniform lighting would remove another source of stimulation, particularly at those times when the children have to be left unattended; even then, it would seem desirable to devise 'situations' – suitable toys and activities – that focused attention on manipulative play and exploration and drew the child outwards from himself.

Implications

Formal observational methods can be expensive in terms of the time and effort required. Observers have to be trained in the techniques of observing and recording, and steps have to be taken to ensure that satisfactory levels of reliability and consistency are maintained by the single observer or among the team of observers. Within the MHVI school or unit, it will usually be the teachers and other care-givers who will be carrying out this work, and they will normally be fulfilling their routine tasks at the same time. Nevertheless, some behaviours may be so unacceptable (because they are self-injurious or disturbing to other children, or preventing the development of important skills) that such expenditure of valuable staff time is justifiable. The circumstances that give rise to them or that reinforce their continuance, can often be pinpointed by careful observation. These methods should therefore be seen as a part of the general assessment methodology to be used by multi-disciplinary teams. They can provide baseline data for evaluating the effectiveness of particular teaching, caring and 'management' programmes, and they have the added advantage that their use involves the participation of all members of the team and family, and not merely those experts who see the child occasionally and for relatively short periods of time.

CHAPTER 6

Blind and Partially Sighted Adults

Rehabilitation and adjustment

As shown in Chapter 1, most people registered as blind or partially sighted are adults aged 65 years and above. Their visual disabilities are in most cases of late onset, with only a very small percentage of the group being congenitally blind or partially sighted. Non-medical assessment has also been mainly concerned with issues to do with the needs of newly blind people of working age. However, the RNIB survey of blind and partially sighted adults in Britain (Bruce *et al.*, 1991) revealed that approximately three-quarters of those in the age range 16–59 years were not in paid employment, and this must raise the question as to whether such assessment is largely superfluous, especially if there are few rehabilitation facilities, programmes or jobs available, or if there are no real alternatives available within these systems. While many changes have occurred in the training and rehabilitation services (see, for example, Hewitt, 1993), the criticism is still made that people are all too often expected to fit into what is on offer from statutory and voluntary bodies rather than having their individual wishes, needs and ambitions addressed during the process of assessment and re-training. Given the poor employment prospects, the whole purpose of formal rehabilitation is perhaps in need of re-evaluation, and this would entail consideration of the how and why of assessment procedures. Dodds, Ng and Yates (1992) have suggested that 'personal rehabilitation' should be given greater attention and that there are many people who could benefit but who are debarred because they are not regarded as having employment potential. They go on to argue that even those who are being assessed for vocational purposes may be so seriously depressed that they are unable to 'carry out a wide range of (vocational) assessment tasks when they are at their lowest psychological ebb'. What these commentators seem to be advocating is that the process of adjustment to blindness should be recognized as an important determinant of successful rehabilitation, and perhaps as even an essential precursor to assessment for vocational purposes. If this is so, then a wider and more exhaustive mode of assessment has to be adopted.

The model being recommended by Dodds (1989; 1991) rests initially upon the notion of the developing of 'self-efficacy', a process in which the client is helped to regain self-confidence and the motivation to acquire new, compensatory skills in, for example, daily living, mobility and communication. Bandura's self-efficacy theory (Bandura, 1977) attempts to be exhaustive by acknowledging the importance of the person himself, of those he identifies with (other visually disabled people, for example), of the professional rehabilitators, and of the setting of relevant and achievable goals. Dodds argues that loss of sight takes from the client his normal range of competencies, and the resulting lack of control over his life leads to demoralization, loss of self-esteem, and anxiety and depression. Rehabilitation and adjustment must go hand in hand, with each reinforcing the other. Dodds and his colleagues have begun to tackle what they call the psychodynamics of adjustment by means of an assessment questionnaire known as the Nottingham Adjustment Scale. Their research has led them to believe that adjustment is

> characterised by: an absence of anxiety and depression; a high level of self-esteem; a high sense of efficacy and control; a positive attitude towards visually handicapped people; an acceptance of responsibility for the future; and a belief that a visual disability, does not mean the end of life as one knows it. (Dodds, 1991)

Using the scale as a before-and-after measurement instrument in a specialist residential rehabilitation unit, Dodds has been able to demonstrate improvement in psychological adjustment and well-being, this improvement presumably arising from what the unit has to offer in terms of the teaching of new skills and from the clients' changing perceptions of their own and their fellow clients' control over their lives. What is of equal significance is the interpretation put upon the deterioration in psychological state of some of the residents. Dodds infers that this points to the fact that for some people 'complete adjustment may take much longer than the time-scale presently set aside for rehabilitation, and that part of the process of getting better initially involves getting worse' (ibid., p.104). The continued development and use of the Nottingham Scale may enable the professional workers and the policy-makers to evaluate alternative schemes — full-time, part-time, residential, domiciliary – more effectively, and thus make better-informed decisions as to which parts of the rehabilitation process should be priority targets for up-grading. If Dodds and his colleagues are right, too little attention is being given at present to factors, such as attitudes, negative feelings and depression, that can interfere with the client's ability to mobilise his learning potential and participate in the planning of a rehabilitation programme specific to his own needs and ambitions.

Mobility

It is no doubt a truism to assert that instruction in independent mobility and orientation skills must start from the particular needs of the individual blind person. This would imply a consideration of his own immediate physical environment, what he wishes to do in that environment, the public and private transport facilities available to him, and, of course, what he brings to the task in terms of mental, physical and sensory abilities. Ideally, the mobility instructor will take all these factors into account before she outlines to her client the various skills that she can teach him. Some mobility techniques – long-cane and the use of guide-dogs – have a more general application, enabling the blind person to travel in unfamiliar environments and to cover much longer distances. Almost inevitably, therefore, this universal applicability has given rise to training programmes of considerable complexity, and the individual's unique and immediate needs take second place, on the not unreasonable grounds that the acquisition of the high-level skills associated with these techniques will allow clients to operate in a wide diversity of environments.

The difficulties encountered by the newly blind adult in learning the skills required by the high-level techniques are increased if there are other sensory and physical disabilities. In assessing a client's suitability for such training, and in agreeing a training programme with him, the instructor must have some measure of his cognitive and perceptual capacities (short-term memory, verbal and non-verbal intelligence, spatial awareness, use of residual vision and hearing), but the practice seems to be for the instructor to have to base her assessment of these factors on direct observation and 'clinical' experience rather than upon more formal and objective methods. Dodds, Beggs and Clark-Carter (1986) have shown that there is little agreement among mobility instructors in their assessment of 'clients' priority for training', and have deplored the fact 'that the assessment which a client receives should be as much dependent upon who is carrying out the assessment as it is upon the client's actual status'. The relatively short period of training provided for aspiring mobility instructors, and the wide-ranging content of the courses, have not always given the trainees enough time and practice in the actual teaching and evaluation of mobility skills; it is not surprising in these circumstances that their assessment of their clients is the product of their own developing and subjective experience rather than of their use of valid and reliable measures of clients' needs and aptitudes. They themselves have not been able to devise and validate such procedures, and their work, valuable though it is, has not been underpinned with sufficient resources to generate the development of universally applicable assessment instruments.

Vocational evaluation

In his 1985 survey, Peterson in the United States argued that in vocational evaluation procedures for the visually impaired, the 'primary focus appears to be on evaluating skills related to compensating for blindness', with relatively little involvement of the clients 'in work samples or other experiential techniques in which their interest and ability to do actual tasks may be observed'. His objection to what he saw as an over-emphasis (rather than a wrong emphasis) on skills related to compensating for the disability was that such a precise focusing 'may give inadequate information related to an individual's job-related characteristics and interests'. What Peterson seems to be arguing for is a procedure encompassing the complementary processes of assessing compensory capabilities and direct observation of ability to accomplish specific job-related tasks. Now while it may be highly desirable to assess by observing the client in an actual job situation, this would be an inordinately lengthy procedure. Not only is there the problem of finding agencies/businesses that would co-operate by providing the necessary facilities or of providing within a rehabilitation centre a whole range of simulated jobs, there is in addition the problem of deciding which of the real jobs or simulated jobs are to be attempted. There must be, to save everybody's time, some system of decision-making that will guide advisers and clients to a manageable set of desirable and realistic job choices. And this brings us back to the need for an assessment procedure consisting of aptitude and achievement tests that are good predictors of success in particular jobs that require particular skills.

Unfortunately, it cannot yet be said that we have a comprehensive battery of vocational aptitude tests for visually handicapped people that are valid and reliable. All that can be done, therefore, is to draw attention to some of the tests that are available and suggest how they may be used and interpreted.

Manual dexterity and tactual perception

While all assessment of newly blinded adults must be justifiable on the grounds that it will provide information for them and their advisers that will be directly useful for planning individualized rehabilitation and training programmes, there is also some justification for using tests that, although devised for a specific purpose, will allow the adviser in a short time to observe other aspects of functioning and personality. The Purdue Pegboard (a test of manual dexterity) can be used in this way since it allows the experienced observer to note her client's willingness to use any residual vision; his general speed, mode of attack and approach to problem solving; his handedness; and his general motivation and teachability.

As a structured method of observation (with the inferences being cross-checked with other information), the Purdue has much in its favour. It was designed originally to enable comparisons to be made among groups of sighted workers and applicants for work. In a study carried out in the United States with blind people to predict manual work success, Hoffman (1958) found that performance on the Purdue was significantly correlated with earnings. Other investigators had found massive differences between the scores of various groups of visually impaired subjects and the Purdue norms for the fully sighted. These not unsurprising results bring out quite starkly the difficulty for people with severe degrees of visual impairment of manipulative tasks involving gross movements of hand, fingers and arms, and finer movements requiring fingertip dexterity. To assess the extent to which even small amounts of residual vision may facilitate accomplishment on tasks of this nature, Tobin and Greenhalgh (1987) administered the test to nearly one thousand newly blind and partially sighted adults who were undergoing vocational rehabilitation in the UK. There are four sets of skills, all timed. Three require the insertion of small steel pins into columns of holes in a wooden board with each hand in turn and then both hands working simultaneously, and the fourth consists of assembling pins, collars and washers with both hands working in an alternating sequence. Tobin and Greenhalgh (ibid., p.75) adopted the three-trial method, first of all to ensure greater reliability in the obtained scores, and secondly to encourage other assessors, in the clinical situation, to observe changes in their clients' short-term learning and motivation from one trial to the next. No attempt was made to prevent the use of residual vision, since this would allow its effects to be measured and would again encourage assessors to try to learn something about clients' near vision and their willingness to use it.

Figure 6.1 brings out the superiority of the female subjects on all sub-tasks, and the beneficial effects of higher levels of visual acuity. The investigators report other statistical data so that users can make multiple comparisons: as between sighted and visually impaired subjects, between men and women, and between subjects with the same and with different degrees of residual vision. Take, for example, a woman adventiously blinded in adult life, and left with perception of hand movements; if she obtained a raw score of 84 on the assembly task she would be placed at the 50th centile against the norms for visually handicapped women. In other words, she would be superior to 50 per cent of such women and her performance would be classified as just 'average'. When compared, however, with others in Group 2 (perception of hand movements, women), it would be seen that her score was one standard deviation above the mean, and would therefore be well above average for that particular group. Her performance on this task would, in fact, be almost equivalent to that of a woman of average ability in Group 4 (1/60 to 3/60 Snellen), i.e. two vision groups above her own; it would also put her at a point equal to men in Group 5, i.e. with vision in the 3/60 to 6/60 Snellen category.

The Tobin and Greenhalgh investigation thus enables the experienced professional worker to make these multiple comparisons and then to discuss with a client some of the implications that his current level of achievement may have for his choice of training courses. This, together with the inferences drawn from actual observation of how the task was tackled, could prove of value to examiner and client.

Researchers have explored various methods of assessing tactual perception skills. Some have used textured surfaces such as sandpaper, and others have used callipers for measuring the minimum distance apart before two stimuli can no longer be sensed as separate. None of these procedures has resulted in a standardized test that can be used by practitioners to guide them in making decisions as to how and whether braille (or an alternative tactile code such as the Moon script) should be taught to a newly blind adult. Instead, the usual practice is to allow the adult learner to make a start on the learning of braille and then for him to discuss with the tutor/adviser whether or not to continue with the course. This is, superficially at least, a praiseworthy approach in that it

Figure 6.1 Graphic Representation of Mean Scores for Six Visually Impaired Groups on Tasks Involving Manual Dexterity (First Published in the *British Journal of Occupational Psychology,* 1987, 60, 73-80).

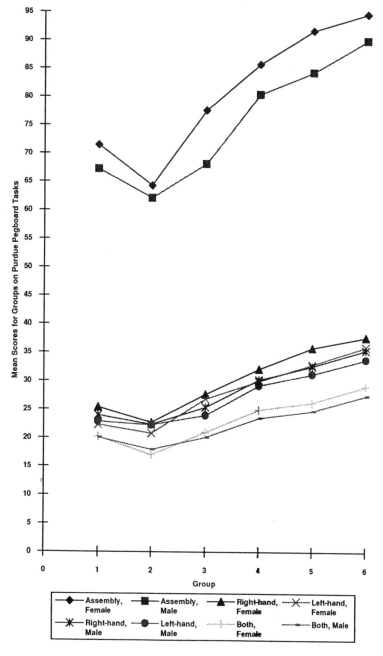

gives control to the client. However, the initial difficulties encountered with the braille code are probably the worst, and learners may be underestimating their capacity to overcome the tactile and intellectual demands made by braille.

In the absence of tests that are good predictors of successful learning, an 'assessment through teaching/learning' approach is recommended. In this kind of system, the learner is being assessed as he learns, and while the final decision to persevere must be left to him the devising of learning sequences by the tutor takes account of immediate success or failure, with tasks being made more or less difficult according to the learner's progress. In braille, the tactile demands can be altered to some extent by varying the size of the braille cell, the spacing between words, and the spacing between lines. Observation of the ease and speed at which the learner copes with these changing demands can be used by the experienced tutor as the basis of the advice she offers her client as to whether the learning of braille should be continued. This is still of course mainly a subjective assessment, and open to the charge made by Dodds *et al.* (1986) about mobility assessment being too dependent upon who is carrying out the evaluation.

In making the decision to proceed with what may be a prolonged period of learning, the client can be helped by having possible options explained to him. Some may want, for achieving other learning objectives, to persevere with the mastery of fully contracted Standard English Braille. Others may wish to be able to do no more than label household utensils and food containers so that they can identify these items without recourse to sighted friends and relatives; for them, an uncontracted form of braille may be sufficient, with the teaching/learning being directed towards tactual recognition of a limited range of words and to the use of the braille writing devices that will enable them to produce their own labels, shopping lists and cooking recipes.

Some practitioners try to assess a client's aptitude for tactual reading by using the Moon system. The tactile symbols are larger than their counterparts in braille and are therefore easier to identify. Moreover, the close similarity of the Moon symbols to printed text is a positive advantage, reducing the learning and memory load. The newly blind adult who finds even this system at the limit of his tactual perception ability is likely to find the smaller braille cells impossible to discriminate from one another. Nevertheless, because tactual perception skills, unlike basic tactual acuity, seem to be capable of development through practice, some teachers believe that growing competence in Moon may enable the learner to transfer to braille. The larger library of texts available in braille than in Moon script makes transfer a desirable goal to work towards, as does the wider range of devices for writing braille.

The assessment through teaching/learning approach is the one adopted by teachers who assess aptitude for using some of the modern technological devices such as the Optacon. The Optacon, through an array of vibrating rods, converts ink-print directly into a tactile form that can be felt by the finger pad. Being a lightweight, easily portable machine, the Optacon immediately opens up for the blind reader a wide range of text materials not available in braille or Moon. It has been found, however, that above-average tactual ability, like that possessed by good braillists, is necessary if the output of the Optacon is to be sensed and decoded accurately and swiftly. For the newly blind client, who has not learned braille, assessment for training on the Optacon can only be done with the device itself. (This procedure has what is called 'face validity'; that is, the testing seems to be measuring the skills that are directly related to the task to be mastered. 'Predictive validity', on the other hand, refers to the ability of a test to predict achievement on a task that may or may not have the same content as the test battery; verbal intelligence may, for example, have some useful predictive validity in relation to the learning of braille, Moon or the Optacon, although the test may not consist of tasks that are identical to those involved in reading braille or reading print with the Optacon.)

Clients' rating of their needs

When it comes to assessing needs, as opposed to abilities or aptitudes, then the client's own perception of those needs is, or should be, the main focus of attention. Of course, in all rehabilitation centres it is routine practice to question the clients about their aspirations, and this, inevitably, will reveal the information about what they percieve as the requirements that will enable them to achieve their goals.

Some useful work in this area has been carried out at the Central Blind Rehabilitation Center at the United States Veterans Administration Hospital (Schulz *et al.*, 1985). The procedure developed by the Americans consists of 'an activities questionnaire' with sections on self-care, home-care, travel, recreation, writing and reading. In essence, intensity of need is measured by how much time the client is willing to spend on further training to improve performance, and four questions are asked, concerned with frequency, difficulty, satisfaction and motivation.

As indicated, motivation to learn a given skill is measured by the amount of time the client would be willing to devote to further training. If, of course, he rates the activity as easy for him to do and he is satisfied with his level of skill, the fourth question is not asked. The responses to the 70 or so items in the questionnaire can also be ranked so that the rehabilitation agency can obtain an overall picture of the client's perceived needs and then discuss with him the order of priority to be attached to each area.

It will be observed that it is the agency that has drawn up the list of skills/activities, and this does not guarantee that we have in fact an overview of all the client's perceived needs; in other words, it is *not* an open-ended questionnaire as it stands, but there is no reason why the client should not be asked to mention any needs not referred to in the list. The same four questions could then be posed vis-à-vis these client-defined needs. In addition, the staff of any rehabilitation centre could add to, or delete from, the list as originally devised, so that it accords more closely with their own experience of client needs and/or the centre's own training programmes and facilities. The procedure as described seems likely to be useful and informative. What it would appear to elicit is information about general care, social and cognitive skills that would be fundamental for, pre-requisites of, a whole range of 'higher level' competences. It does not, however, tell us whether a client would be able, for example, to take up, or cope with training for, the job of welfare officer, teacher, secretary, computer programmer, psychologist, lathe operator, etc. It tells us nothing, then, about aptitude for a particular job.

The underlying concept of this activities/skills questionnaire is capable of extension in a number of ways. One such way would consist of applying the questions (modified as appropriate) during job and task demonstration, try-outs and simulations. For example, one could use it after the blind person has had half-an-hour's 'hands-on' experience with an Optacon, a Kurzweil machine, the Possum Moon-writer or a micro-computer-based word-processing system. The procedure would not disclose aptitude for mastering a given learning task or technological device, but it could be part of the overall procedure and would demonstrate to the client that he himself is being actively engaged in the decision-making process concerning career guidance and further training programmes.

Print reading adults

Many adults registered as blind, and all who are partially sighted, have vision that may be adequate for reading print. In many cases, reading will require magnifiers or other low vision aids (LVAs), some of which are expensive. Assessment of the possible value of LVAs to an individual is an undertaking that falls within the responsibility of qualified ophthalmic opticians and optometrists, who have to take into account visual acuity, visual fields, contrast sensitivity and the highly specific educational and vocational needs of the client within a given and often unique lighting environment. Unfortunately, there is anecdotal evidence suggesting that many elderly adults and even some visually impaired adults of working age are not being routinely assessed to determine whether an LVA would be of assistance to them, a situation that was being highlighted by Silver and colleagues in the 1970s when they reported that no more than 31 per cent of employment rehabilitation clients had had an LVA assessment (Silver *et al.*, 1974).

More informal assessment procedures have been pioneered by the Partially Sighted Society in the UK. Clients are given the opportunity to experiment with different kinds of aids, and are assisted by low vision therapists who work alongside the client and who give instruction not only in how best to use the aids but also in how to use whatever residual vision they may have. Given the cost and relative sophistication of some devices – closed circuit television magnifiers and computer controlled visual display units, for example – assessment should take note of the learner's motivation and the general acceptability of the aids. Cosmetic factors and the space and other requirements in a workplace are not easily assessed in the laboratory or clinic. To that extent, therefore, informal or subjective evaluation has a part to play.

The assessment of low-vision clients in other aspects of functioning is often possible with tests devised for the fully sighted. The British Picture Vocabulary Scale (BPVS) was described in Chapter 3 and the case was made for it as a means not only of measuring vocabulary but also as a method for informal observation of the subject's use of his vision. The Scale (Dunn *et al.*, 1982) is a measure of listening vocabulary, acquired vocabulary being itself a part of more general verbal intelligence. It has been standardized on a large sample of British schoolchildren and young adults, and its ease and speed of administration make it a useful tool for rehabilitation professionals, teachers and social workers, but, as pointed out in Chapter 3, low scores by visually impaired subjects on this test cannot be given the same credence as high scores. Very poor

94

sight can interfere with the subject's ability to decipher the drawings, even though his vocabulary skills may be of a high order.

If a psychologist is assessing non-cognitive factors such as personality traits and characteristics, then the Cattell 16 Personality Factor Questionnaire (Cattell *et al.*, 1970) has the added advantage of being able, via its Factor B, to provide an estimate of intelligence. A more comprehensive estimate of verbal and non-verbal intelligence would require the use of an instrument such as the Wechsler Adult Intelligence Scale, the administration and interpretation of which needs a qualified psychologist.

Other vocational interest assessment procedures

There are various British instruments available to assess vocational interests and preferences. However, caution is needed not only when trying to interpret the results, but also in their actual administration. Most were designed for fully sighted clients to complete themselves. With adventitiously blinded and partially sighted adults, that is, of course, not possible, but ways can be found for tape-recording the instructions and for the clients to select alternatives by simple embossing or by the sorting into piles of cards or tallies, thus making it possible for privacy to be maintained. The difficulty with the most obvious of the other modifications, viz. oral administration and scoring by a sighted counsellor, is that one cannot be sure that the counsellor's mere presence is not affecting or biasing the client's responses. Among the British tests that can be used in this way (all published by NFER-NELSON) are:

(1)   Self Directed Search, by J.L. Holland. This tool is said to allow clients to answer questions about 'their occupational daydreams and preferred and disliked interests and occupations'. The client and counsellor can use the ensuing profile for pinpointing suitable jobs from a list of 1,100 occupations.

(2)   The Rothwell-Miller Interest Blank, by K.M. Miller. This lists some 200 job titles arranged in blocks of 12, with the client being required to put in rank order of preference the jobs within each block. Scores can then be computed for a dozen areas of interest — outdoors, mechanical, scientific, social services, persuasive, computational, aesthetic, literary, musical, practical and medical.

(3)   The Vocational Preference Inventory, by J.L. Holland. This instrument has eleven scales — realistic, intellectual, social, conventional, enterprising, artistic, self-control, masculinity,

status, infrequency and acquiescence. It will be seen to differ from the other Holland test (the Self Directed Search) in that it yields information about underlying personality traits, values and coping behaviours.

(4) The Strong–Campbell Interest Inventory, by E.K. Strong and D. Campbell. This inventory provides a graphic representation of an individual's interest in six occupational themes – enterprising, artistic, realistic, social, conventional, investigative – and covers some 160 occupations. All the client has to do is to answer 'Like', 'Indifferent', 'Dislike' to a large number of jobs, activities and amusements. Responses are compared with those of successful people in various types of work.

(5) The Work Aspect Preference Scale, by R.G.L. Pryor. This questionnaire focuses upon those qualities that a person considers worthwhile and rewarding in a job.

The major concern one would have about these instruments is that they have not been constructed for use with newly blinded or newly partially sighted adults. They pre-suppose, therefore, that consideration of the whole range of possible jobs is open, in principle at least, to the clients and their advisers. Clearly, this is not the case. Blind adults will not be accepted for training as engine drivers, airline stewardesses, traffic wardens or postmen. They have not, also, been standardized on a population of people who are in the process of adjusting to a disability such as blindness. The newly blinded are not the same as the congenitally blinded nor as the adventitiously blinded who have gone through the various – sometimes very lengthy – phases of acceptance and rehabilitation. These instruments should, therefore, be seen as structured methods of observing and assessing the client, but the scores and profiles obtained at the end of assessment must be treated with care. With care, not only because they may not be as 'reliable' as one would wish (on account of the inadequate standardization with a visually disabled sample) but unreliable because the person we are observing may himself be in the process of some quite major changes in personality, self-esteem, and hope and expectations about his future life. Nevertheless, newly blinded adults are adult human beings, the attributes they have in common with their fully sighted fellows being much greater and being more significant than the characteristics that now differentiate them from their sighted peers.

APPENDIX

Glossary of Some Commonly Used Words Related to Visual Impairment and Disability

Accommodation
The adjustment in the curvature of the eye for seeing at different distances, accomplished by changing the shape of the **crystalline lens** through the action of the ciliary muscles, thus bringing objects into focus.

Acuity (visual)
The power of the eye to distinguish the form and shape (as opposed to the colour) of objects that are in the direct line of vision; the ability to distinguish very fine detail; different measures are made of **distance vision** and **near vision**.

Amblyopia
Weak sight with or without any specific disease of the eye.

Binocular vision
The ability to use both eyes simultaneously to focus on the same object and to *fuse* the two images into a single image which gives a correct interpretation of its solidity and position in space.

Blindness
The official definition in Great Britain of a blind person is 'a person so blind as to be unable to perform any work for which eyesight is essential'. Visual **acuity** of 3/60 or less in the better eye usually constitutes blindness. However, where an individual's **field of vision** is markedly contracted, then a visual acuity of more than 3/60 can constitute blindness. For *educational* purposes, the Education Act of 1944 defined blind pupils as those with no sight or those whose sight is

or is likely to become, so defective that they may require education by methods not involving the use of sight.

Cataract
Opacity of the lens of the eye, leading to loss of visual **acuity**.

Choroid
Middle coat of the eyeball containing blood vessels and pigment cells.

Colour blindness
Diminished ability to see differences in colour.

Cones and rods
Two kinds of cells which form a layer of the **retina** and act as light-receiving media. Cones are concerned with visual **acuity** and colour discrimination; rods with motion and vision at low degrees of illumination (night vision).

Cornea
The transparent part of the outer wall of the eyeball.

Crystalline lens
A transparent, colourless body suspended behind the **iris**, the function of which is to bring the rays of light to a focus on the **retina**.

Distance vision
A person's vision as measured by **Snellen** and similar tests. It refers to the resolving power of the eye when looking at an object over six metres from the eye when the **accommodation** mechanism is at rest.

Field of vision
The monocular area from 60 degrees nasally to 180 degrees temporally – the entire area which can be seen without shifting the gaze.

Fovea
Small depression in the **retina**. Part of the **macula** adapted for most acute vision.

Fusion
The power of co-ordinating the images received by the two eyes into a single image or impression.

Hemianopia
Loss of half the **field of vision**.

Iris
Coloured circular membrane suspended behind the **cornea** and immediately in front of the lens, serving to regulate the amount of light entering the eye by changing the size of the pupil.

Ishihara colour plates
A test for defects in recognizing colours, based on the ability to perceive patterns in a series of multi-coloured plates.

Light perception
Ability to distinguish light from dark.

Light projection
Ability to detect the source of origin of light.

Low vision aids (LVAs)
Any optical appliance that does more than correct a **refraction error**. There are two main types in current use; those which are hand-held or hand-manipulated and those worn (as in a spectacle frame).

Macula
The small area of the **retina** that surrounds the **fovea** and comprises the area of distinct vision.

Myopia (nearsightedness)
A **refraction error** in which (because the globe is too long in relation to its focusing power) the point of focus for rays of light from distant objects is in front of the **retina**. Myopic individuals can read at their near point without distance correction.

N print test
A test of **near vision** using cards of different sizes of print held by the reader at any distance convenient for him. Starting with the largest

print, the reader reads progressively smaller print until the smallest print that he can read has been reached.

Near point of accommodation
The nearest point at which the eye can focus an object distinctly. It varies according to the power of **accommodation**.

Near vision
The ability to perceive distinctly objects at normal reading distance, or about 14 inches from the eyes.

Nystagmus
Involuntary movements of the eyeball. There are various kinds: lateral, vertical, rotatory and mixed.

Optic atrophy
Degeneration of the optic nerve that carries messages from the **retina** to the brain.

Partial sight (Great Britain)
A partially sighted person is defined as one who is 'substantially or permanently handicapped by defective vision caused by congenital defect, or illness, or injury', but not 'so blind as to be unable to perform any work for which eyesight is essential'. Visual **acuity** of between 6/60 and 6/18 with good or contracted fields can constitute partial sight. The educational definition of partial sight refers to 'pupils who by reason of defective vision cannot follow the ordinary curriculum without detriment to their sight or to their educational development, but can be educated by special methods involving the use of sight'.

Peripheral vision
Ability to perceive the presence, motion or colour of objects outside the direct line of vision; perception by the whole **retina** excluding the **macula**.

Refraction errors
Defects or irregularities in the eye producing distorted images on the **retina**.

Residual vision
The amount of vision a visually impaired individual has left; a term lacking in precision but widely used in discussion of an individual's ability to use his limited vision for various purposes.

Retina
A membrane of highly complex structure, lining the innermost surface of the eye, formed of sensitive nerve fibres and connected to the optic nerve. It collects visual stimuli whose impulses are transmitted by the optic nerve to the brain where the retinal image is coded and categorized.

Retinal detachment
Separation of **retina** from the **choroid**, leading to reduction or absence of vision.

Scotoma
A blind or partially blind area in the visual field.

Snellen test
A distance test of central visual **acuity**. It consists of lines of letters, numbers or symbols in graded sizes. Each line is labelled with the distance at which it can be read by the normal eye. A reading of 6/6 means the individual has 'normal' vision, i.e. he can read at six metres what most people are able to read at six metres. Gradations on the Snellen Chart are normally in multiples of 6: 6/6 (normal vision), 6/12, 6/18, 6/24, 6/36, 6/60 are progressively worse readings.

Tunnel vision
Contraction of the **field of vision** to such an extent that only a small area of central visual **acuity** remains, thus giving the affected individual the impression of looking through a tunnel.

References

Aitken, S. and Buultjens, M. (1992) *Vision for Doing. Assessing Functional Vision of Learners Who are Multiply Disabled.* Edinburgh: Moray House Publications.

Bandura, A. (1977) 'Self-efficacy: toward a unifying theory of behavioural change'. *Psychological Review*, 84, 191–215.

Barraga, N.C. (1964) *Increased Visual Behaviour in Low Vision Children.* New York: American Foundation for the Blind.

Barraga, N.C. (1970) *Teacher's Guide for Development of Visual Learning Abilities and Utilization of Low Vision.* Louisville: American Printing House for the Blind.

Bate, M. and Smith, M. (1986) *Assessment in Nursery Education.* Windsor: NFER-NELSON.

Bellman, M. and Cash, J. (1987) *The Schedule of Growing Skills.* Windsor: NFER-NELSON.

Best, T. and Bell, J. (1984) 'Assessment of children with profound handicaps: an analysis of schedules'. *Mental Handicap*, December 1984, 12, 160–3.

Bone, M. and Meltzer, H. (1989) *OPCS Surveys of Disability in Great Britain, Report 3: The Prevalence of Disability Among Children.* London: HMSO.

Bradley-Johnson, S. (1986) *Psychoeducational Assessment of Visually Impaired and Blind Students.* Austin, Texas: Pro-ed.

Brown, D., Simmons, V. and Methvin, J. (1986) *The Oregon Project for Visually Impaired and Blind Pre-school Children* (3rd edition). Medford, Oregon: Jackson County Education Service Department.

Bruce, I., McKennell, A. and Walker, E. (1991) *Blind and Partially Sighted Adults in Britain: The RNIB Survey* (Volume 1). London: HMSO.

Cattell, R.B., Ever, H.W. and Tatsuoka, M.M. (1970) *Handbook for* the Sixteen Personality Factor Questionnaire (16PF). Windsor: NFER Publishing Co. Ltd.

Chapman, E.K., Tobin, M.J., Tooze, F.H. and Moss, S. (1989) Look and Think: A Handbook for Teachers. Visual Perception Training for Visually Impaired Children (5–11 years) (2nd edition, revised). London: Royal National Institute for the Blind.

Clamp, S. (1988) An Investigation into the Mathematical Understanding of Number Operations, Fractions, Measurements, and Algebra by Visually Handicapped Children Aged 11–15 Years. Birmingham: University of Birmingham, unpublished M.Ed. thesis.

Daly, B., Addington, J., Kerfoot, S. and Sigston, A. (1985) Portage: The Importance of Parents. Windsor: NFER-NELSON.

van Dijk, J. (1971) 'Learning difficulties and deaf/blind children'. In: Proceedings of the Fourth International Conference on Deaf/Blind Children. Watertown, Mass: Perkins School for the Blind.

Dodds, A.G. (1989) 'Motivation reconsidered: the importance of self-efficacy in rehabilitation'. British Journal of Visual Impairment, VII, 1, 11–15.

Dodds, A.G. (1991) 'The psychology of rehabilitation.' British Journal of Visual Impairment, 9, 2, 38–40.

Dodds, A.G., Beggs, W.D.A. and Clark-Carter, D. (1986) 'Client assessment (mobility training)'. British Journal of Visual Impairment, IV, 2, 53–7.

Dodds, A.G., Ng, L. and Yates, L. (1992) 'Residential rehabilitation. 2 – Psychological outcome of rehabilitation'. The New Beacon, LXXVI, 902, 373–7.

DOH (1991) Registered Blind and Partially Sighted People at 31st March, 1991, England. A/F 91/7. London: Department of Health.

Doll, E.A. (1953) Measurement of Social Competence. A Manual for the Vineland Social Maturity Scale. Minnesota: American Guidance Service, Inc.

Donlon, E.T. and Curtis, W.S. (1972) The Development and Evaluation of a Video-taped Protocol for the Examination of Multi-handicapped Deaf/Blind Children. Final Report. Syracuse, NY: Syracuse University.

Dunn, L., Dunn, L., Whetton, C. and Pintilie, D. (1982) British Picture Vocabulary Scale. Windsor: NFER-NELSON.

Elliott, C.D. (1990) Differential Ability Scales. Introductory and Technical Handbook. San Antonio, Texas: The Psychological Corporation, Harcourt Brace Jovanovich.

Elliott, C.D. Murray, D.J. and Pearson, L.S. (1983) British Ability Scales. Windsor: NFER-NELSON.

Ellis, D. (1986) *Sensory Impairment in Mentally Handicapped People.* London: Croom Helm.

Fletcher, R. (1980) *City University Colour Vision Test.* London: Messrs Keller Ltd.

Foster, B.M. (1973) *A Review of Literature: Aspects of Visual Handicap with a Comparative Study of the Visual Efficiency of Sighted and Partially Sighted Children at Ages 6 – 7.5 and 9 – 10.5 as Measured on the Barraga Visual Efficiency Scale.* Birmingham: University of Birmingham, unpublished M.Ed. (Educ. Psych.) dissertation.

Gillman, A.E. and Goddard, D.R. (1974) 'The 20-year outcome of blind children two years old and younger: a preliminary survey'. *New Outlook for the Blind*, January, 1974, 68, 1, 1 – 7.

Gipps, C., Gross, H. and Goldstein, H. (1987) *Warnock's Eighteen Per Cent. Children with Special Needs in Primary Schools.* Lewes: The Falmer Press.

Gomulicki, B.R. (1961) *The Development of Perception and Learning in Blind Children.* Cambridge: University of Cambridge Psychological Laboratory (*mimeo*).

Guess, D. (1967) 'Mental retardation and blindness: a complex and relatively unexplored dyad'. *Exceptional Children*, 33, 7, 471 – 9.

Harley R. and Spollen, J. (1973) 'A study of the reliability and validity of the Visual Efficiency Scale with low vision children'. *Education of the Visually Handicapped*, 5, 4, 110 – 14.

Harley, R., Spollen, J. and Long, S. (1973) 'A study of the reliability and validity of the Visual Efficiency Scale with pre-school children'. *Education of the Visually Handicapped*, 5, 2, 38 – 42.

Hart, K.M. (1980) *Secondary School Children's Understanding of Mathematics.* Research Monograph. London: Centre for Science Education, Chelsea College, University of London.

Hayes, S.P. (1941) *Contributions to a Psychology of Blindness.* New York: American Foundation for the Blind.

Hewitt, B. (1993) 'Assessment and rehabilitation at RNIB Manor House'. *The New Beacon*, LXXVII, 912, 341 – 6.

Hoffman, S. (1958) 'Some predictors of the manual work success of blind persons'. *Personnel and Guidance Journal*, 36, 542 – 4.

Holmes, S. (1992) 'Selecting an assessment instrument for use with adults with a profound mental handicap and multiple impairments'. *Mental Handicap*, 20, 3, 90 – 6.

Hull, T. and Mason, H. (1993) 'The Speed of Information Processing Test for the blind in a tactile version'. *British Journal of Visual Impairment*, 11, 1, 21 – 3.

Hyvarinen, L. and Lindstedt, E. (1981) *Assessment of Vision in Children.* Stockholm: The Authors.

Kiernan, C.C. (1987) 'Criterion-referenced tests'. In: Hogg, J. and Raynes, N.V. (eds), *Assessment in Mental Handicap: A Guide to Assessment Practices, Tests, and Checklists.* London: Croom Helm.

Kiernan, C.C. and Jones, L.M. (1982) *Behaviour Assessment Battery: Assessment of the Cognitive, Communicative, and Self-help Skills of Severely Handicapped Children* (2nd edition). Windsor: NFER-NELSON.

Koestler, F. (1976) *The Unseen Minority: A Social History of Blindness in the United States.* New York: David McKay Co.

Langley, M.B. (1986) 'Psychoeducational assessment of visually impaired students with additional handicaps'. In: Ellis, D. (ed.), *Sensory Impairments in Mentally Handicapped People.* London: Croom Helm.

Lorimer, J. (1962) *The Lorimer Braille Recognition Test.* Bristol: College of Teachers of the Blind (now available from the Association for the Education and Welfare of the Visually Handicapped).

Lorimer, J. (1977) *Neale Analysis of Reading Ability Adapted for Use with Blind Children. Manual of Directions and Norms.* Windsor: National Foundation for Educational Research.

Mason, H.L. and Shukla, S.R. (1992) 'The use of the Blind Learning Aptitude Test in England and Wales, India, and the USA'. *British Journal of Visual Impairment*, 10, 3, 95 – 9.

Mason, H. and Tobin, M.J. (1986) 'Speed of information processing and the visually handicapped child'. *British Journal of Special Education*, 13, 2, 69 – 70.

Maxfield, K.E. and Buchholz, S. (1957) *A Social Maturity Scale for Blind Pre-school Children: A Guide to its Use.* New York: American Foundation for the Blind.

Neale, M.D. (1958) *Neale Analysis of Reading Ability: Manual of Directions and Norms* (2nd edition, 1966). London: MacMillan.

Neale, M.D. (1989) *Neale Analysis of Reading Ability* (revised British edition). Windsor: NFER-NELSON.

Newland, T.E. (1971) *The Blind Learning Aptitude Test.* Champaign, Ill.: University of Illinois Press.

Nolan, C.Y. (1959) 'Achievement in arithmetic computation'. *International Journal for the Education of the Blind*, 8, 4, 125 – 8.

Peterson, M. (1985) 'Vocational evaluation of blind and visually impaired persons for technical, professional, and managerial positions'. *Journal of Visual Impairment and Blindness*, 79, 10, 478 – 80.

Reynell, J. (1979) *Manual for the Reynell-Zinkin Scales. Developmental Scales for Young Visually Handicapped Children: Part 1, Mental Development.* Windsor: NFER-NELSON.

Schulz, E.M., Ross, W.L., Becker, S.W., Wright, B.D. and Bezruczko, M.A. (1985) 'An assessment of the needs of rehabilitated veterans'. *Journal of Visual Impairment and Blindness,* 79, 7, 301–5.

Sebba, J. (1978) *A System for Assessment and Intervention for Pre-school Profoundly Retarded Multiply Handicapped Children.* M.Ed. thesis. Manchester: University of Manchester.

Sheridan, M. (1976) *Manual for the Stycar Vision Tests.* Windsor: NFER.

Sheridan, M.D. and Gardiner, P.A. (1970) 'Sheridan-Gardiner Test for Visual Acuity'. *British Medical Journal,* 2, 108–9.

Silver, J., Gould, E. and Thomsett, J. (1974) 'The provision of low vision aids to the visually handicapped'. *Transactions of the Ophthalmology Society of the UK,* 94, 310–18.

Simon, G.B. (1986) *The Next Step on the Ladder: Assessment and Management of Children with Multiple Handicaps* (4th edition). Kidderminster: British Institute of Mental Handicap.

Sims, A.M. (1967) '"Modern" mathematics in secondary school'. In: *The Teaching of Science and Mathematics to the Blind.* London: Royal National Institute for the Blind.

Sonksen, P.M. and Macrae, A.J. (1987) 'Vision for coloured pictures at different acuities: the Sonksen Picture Guide to Visual Function'. *Developmental Medicine and Child Neurology,* 29, 337–47.

Stockley, J. and Richardson, P. (1991) *Profile of Adaptive Skills. A Rating Scale for Assessing Progressive Personal and Social Development in Young People with Visual Impairment in Association with Moderate to Severe Learning Difficulties.* London: Royal National Institute for the Blind.

Tiffin, J. (1968) *Purdue Pegboard: Examiner Manual.* Chicago: Science Research Associates.

Tobin, M.J. (1972) 'A study in the improvement of visual efficiency in children registered as blind'. *New Beacon,* LVI, 659, 58–60.

Tobin, M.J. (1978) 'An introduction to the psychological and educational assessment of blind and partially sighted'. In: Portwood, P.F. and Williams, R.T. (eds), *Readings in the Visually Handicapped Child.* DECP Occasional Papers, II, II. Leicester: British Psychological Society.

Tobin, M.J. (1979) 'A longitudinal study of blind and partially sighted children in special schools in England and Wales'. *Insight,* 1, 1, 8–14.

106

Tobin, M.J. and Greenhalgh, R. (1987). 'Normative data for assessing the manual dexterity of visually handicapped adults in vocational rehabilitation'. *Journal of Occupational Psychology*, 60, 73–80.

Tobin, M.J., Hill, R.E., Leary, J. and Simon, G.B. (1972) *Investigations into the Behaviour and Needs of Visually Handicapped and Mentally Retarded Children in an Experimental Residential and Educational Unit.* Birmingham: University of Birmingham, Research Centre for the Education of the Visually Handicapped (*mimeo*).

Tobin, M.J. and Myers, S.O. (1978) *Memory Span Tests for the Deaf-Blind.* Birmingham: University of Birmingham, Research Centre for the Education of the Visually Handicapped (*mimeo*).

Tobin, M.J., Tooze, F.H.G., Chapman, E.K. and Moss, S. (1979) *Look and Think: A Handbook on Visual Perception Training for Severely Visually Handicapped Children.* London: Schools Council/Royal National Institute for the Blind.

Tooze, F.H.G. (1962) *The Tooze Braille Speed Test.* Bristol: College of Teachers of the Blind (now available from the Association for the Education and Welfare of the Visually Handicapped).

Tooze, F.H.G. (1967) 'Mathematics for primary school blind children'. In: *The Teaching of Science and Mathematics.* London: Royal National Institute for the Blind.

Tyler, S. (1980) *Keele Pre-school Assessment Guide.* Windsor: NFER-NELSON.

Walker, E., Tobin, M.J. and McKennell, A. (1992) *Blind and Partially Sighted Children in Britain.* The RNIB Survey (Volume 2). London: HMSO.

White, M. and Cameron, R.J. (1988) *Portage: Progress, Problems, and Possibilities.* Windsor: NFER-NELSON.

Whittaker, J. (1967) 'Geographical representation'. In: *The Teaching of Science and Mathematics.* London: Royal National Institute for the Blind.

Williams, M. (1956) *Williams Intelligence Test for Children with Defective Vision.* Windsor: NFER-NELSON.

Wood, P.H.N. (1980) 'The language of disablement: a glossary related to disease and its consequences'. *International Rehabilitation Medicine*, 2, 86–92.

Name Index

Subject Index

110

112

Task Analysis, 27
Teaching Objectives Approach, 25, 27
Tests,
advisability of presenting visual and tactile versions, 8-9
alternative methods of presentation, 62
and assessment through teaching/learning, 90-91
dearth of, xii, 52, 58-59
devised for sighted people, xiii, 52-58, 94-95
for partially sighted, 50, 52-58
for pre-school children, 11-12, 27-38
of braille reading, xiii, 40, 46-53
of intelligence (verbal and non-verbal, memory), 29, 40-46, 72-76
of manual dexterity, xi
of visual perception skills, 15-19
reliability, 4, 16, 20, 34, 40, 45-46, 48, 50, 69, 82, 87, 95
standardised, criticisms of, x, xi, xii
tactile, 42-46
timed, 38, 55-58, 60-61, 87
validity, 4, 16, 20, 34, 45, 69, 72, 95
(see also Language, Multiple Handicap, Self-rating Social Behaviour, Visual Acuity)
The Next Step on the Ladder, 67-69
Time Sampling (see Observation (formal methods))
Tooze Braille Speed Test, 47-50
Tunnel Vision, 100

Validity (see Tests)

Vineland Social Maturity Scale, 28
Vision for Doing: Assessing Functional Vision of Learners who are Multiply Disabled, 69-70
Visual Acuity (see also Blindness, Partial Sight)
and colour blindness, ix
and distance vision, 97
and near vision, 98
definition of, 1, 11, 96
measurement of, 11-12, 21-24
Visual Crowding, 12, 22
Visual Display Units (VDUs) (see also Low Vision Aids), 14-15
Visual Field
and tunnel vision, 100
definition of, 12-13, 97, 98
formal and informal methods of assessing, 13
Visual Perception
definition of, 15
methods of assessing, 15-19
Visual Scanning, 15, 67
Vocational Evaluation and Skills, 72, 86, 91-92, 94-95
Vocational Preference Inventory, 94-95

Wechsler Intelligence Scale for Children (WISC), 44
Wechsler Adult Intelligence Scale (WAIS), 94
Williams Intelligence Test for Children with Defective Vision, 4, 40-42
Work Aspect Preference Scale, The, 95
World Health Organisation, ix